A.W. Reed

Maori Myths
& Legendary Tales

A.W. Reed

Maori Myths
& Legendary Tales

Illustrated by Dennis Turner

NEW
HOLLAND

This edition published in 1999 by New Holland Publishers (NZ) Ltd
Auckland • Sydney • London • Cape Town

218 Lake Road, Northcote, Auckland, New Zealand
14 Aquatic Drive, Frenchs Forest, NSW 2086, Australia
86 Edgware Road, London, W2 2EA, United Kingdom
80 McKenzie Street, Cape Town 8001, South Africa

First published in 1946 as *Myths and Legends of Maoriland*
by A.H. & A.W. Reed
(reprinted 1947, 1950, 1954, 1957)
Second edition published in 1958
Third enlarged edition with Dennis Turner illustrations published in 1961
(reprinted 1964, 1967, 1971, 1974)

ISBN: 1 877246 10 7

Managing editor: Renée Lang
Cover design: Sue Reidy
Cover illustration: 'Te Wehenga O Rangi Raua Ko Papa' by Cliff Whiting,
mixed media, National Library of New Zealand
Text design and typesetting: Graeme Leather

5 7 9 10 8 6

Printed by McPhersons Printing Group, Australia

Contents

Publisher's Note

First published as *Myths and Legends of Maoriland* in 1946, this classic collection was awarded the Esther Glen medal for the best children's book published in New Zealand, in 1947. A second edition was published in 1958, followed by a third enlarged edition in 1961, which featured the illustrations of artist Dennis Turner. A leading book illustrator of the period (including his own book, *Tangi*), Dennis Turner was also an admired painter and muralist.

It is estimated that in excess of 50 000 copies of *Myths and Legends of Maoriland* have been sold in New Zealand since 1946. This figure does not include sales in the United Kingdom, the United States, Australia and even Russia where, in 1960, it is believed that 300 000 copies of a paperback edition were printed in Moscow.

Author and publisher A.W. Reed was a prolific writer on Maori exploration, mythology, arts and crafts, and of books for education and for children. With his uncle, Sir Alfred Reed, he founded A.H. and A.W. Reed, which went on to become the largest book publishing house in New Zealand and Australia. This company's dynamic publishing programme only ended when the firm was split up and merged with other publishing houses. However, many A.H. and A.W. Reed books remain in print today, published by Reed Publishing and the New Holland group.

The Reed name lives on in today's thriving book trade, not least through the establishment by the Reed Trust of the Lifetime Achievement Award for New Zealand authorship, first recipient Margaret Mahy in 1998, and the Good Publisher Award in 1999.

The illustration on the front cover of this latest edition is a detail taken from Dr Cliff Whiting's mixed media work, *Te Wehenga O Rangi Raua Ko Papa* (1969–74), which hangs at the National Library of New Zealand. It depicts Tane as he separated Ranginui, the Sky-father, and Papatuanuku, the Earth-mother, in one of the best known of the Maori accounts of the creation of the world.

One of Maori art's most highly regarded advocates, Cliff

Whiting is currently the Kaihautū, Museum of New Zealand Te Papa Tongarewa, Wellington. The importance of his achievements was recognised in early 1999 when he received the Order of New Zealand – the country's highest honour.

New Holland Publishers would like to acknowledge Ray Richards, the former vice-chairman and publisher of A.H. and A.W. Reed, whose enthusiasm has been the driving force behind this new edition.

Author's Preface

This book is obviously not intended for the student, nor will anything new be found in its pages. It is an attempt to put into unified form the more popular stories which entertained the old-time Maori. If it fails in its purpose, it will not be the fault of the old legends; yet it must be admitted that they present their difficulties. Maori and Pakeha do not think alike, and the neolithic man is far removed from the sophisticated adult of the twentieth century, though perhaps he is closer to the modern child than we might sometimes suspect. His folk-tales are intertwined with his cosmogony and anthropogeny, his lofty religious beliefs as well as the darker side of primitive life and custom. Some of the stories have been adapted for family readership, and the most esoteric elements of religious belief, which later scholarship and the generosity of elders of the tribes have revealed in recent years, have to be omitted from a collection such as this.

A great deal of interesting material has therefore had to be left out, for the pursuit of personalities of legendary, and in some cases historic, interest might be continued endlessly. No attempt has been made to say anything of the later adventures of those who came to Aotearoa nearly a thousand years ago, for their stories lie closer to the borderland of history than of legend. On the other hand, nothing has been said of many interesting personifications of natural phenomena.

Others have done the work of collection and, as the bibliography will show, this is the fruit of their gleaning. Of those who undertook the real work, the collection of legends direct from the learned elders of the tribes and the transcription of the tales of the common people, especial mention must be made of Sir George Grey, John White, and in more recent years, Elsdon Best, James Cowan and Johannes C. Andersen. A score or two of books have been consulted, and in particular the author wishes to acknowledge the following sources of information: *Polynesian Mythology*, by Sir

George Grey; *The Ancient History of the Maori* (six volumes) by John White; *The Lore of the Whare-wananga*, by S. Percy Smith; *The Maori* (two volumes) and *Maori Religion and Mythology*, by Elsdon Best.

Extracts have been made from earlier publications by the present writer: *Maui* (which is embodied in Chapter Four in its entirety); three small booklets written for children under the general title of *Legends of Maoriland* and out of print for many years; *The Coming of the Maori to Aotearoa* (now appearing with some modifications as part of Chapter 10); *Revenge*, by John White (edited by A.W. Reed); and *Legends of Rotorua*. I am also indebted to Guy Powell for many suggestions, and also for his contribution on the origin of the Maori.

Earlier editions of this book contained many illustrations by W. Dittmer and George Woods. The present edition, which has been revised and enlarged, has been illustrated by Dennis Turner, whose earlier imaginative drawings have appeared in the author's *Legends of Rotorua and the Hot Lakes*. Apart from their artistic merit, they present an accurate picture of the life of the old-time Maori.

This book has been written in the hope that the people of New Zealand may learn to treasure their heritage of ancient story and the further heritage that lies within the stories and at their own back doors, the heritage of forests and birds, insects and fish and everything that has been given by the bountiful hand of Tane, the old-time god of the great out-of-doors.

A. W. Reed
Wellington
1961

1

Heaven and Earth

In the far-off time before there was night or day, sun or moon, green fields or golden sand, Rangi the Sky-father lay in the arms of Papa the Earth-mother. For long ages they clung together and their children groped their way blindly between them. There was no light in the world where the children of Rangi and Papa lived, and they longed for freedom, for winds that would blow over the hill-tops and light that would warm their pale bodies.

The closeness of this narrow world at last became unbearable, and the sons of Earth and Sky met together, crawling through the narrow tunnels and caves of their land. They sat down where a few trees sprawled against the sky, twisting their branches into strange shapes.

"What shall we do?" asked the Children of the Gods. "Shall we kill our Father and Mother and let in the light? Or shall we force them apart? We must do something, for we are no longer babies clinging to our mother's body."

"Let us kill them," said Tu-matauenga.

Tane stood up and straightened himself until his head pressed against the hanging sky. "No," he cried, "we cannot kill them. They are Father and Mother to us. Let us force them apart. Let us throw the Sky away and live close to the heart of our Mother." This he said because he was the god of trees that are nourished in the soil.

His brothers murmured their approval – all except Tawhiri-matea, the father of the winds. His voice whistled shrilly as he faced his brother.

"This is an idle thought," he said fiercely. "We are hidden here in safety where nothing can harm us. Out of your own mouth came the words: 'They are our Father and Mother.' Be careful, Tane, for this is a deed of shame."

His words were drowned by the other gods crying aloud in the confined space. "We need light," they said. "We need more room to stretch our cramped limbs. We need the freedom of space."

They brushed past Tawhiri, while Rongo-ma-tane, the father of cultivated food, pressed his shoulders against the Sky-father and tried to straighten himself. In the darkness they could hear his breath, fast and heavy, but there was no movement in the body of Rangi, and the darkness hung heavily round the gods. Then Tangaroa, the father of the sea, of fish and reptiles, put out his strength. Then followed Haumia-tiketike, father of the wild berries and the fern-root, and after him Tu-matauenga, the god of war and father of man. Their efforts were all in vain.

Last of all, Tane-mahuta, the mighty father of the forest, of birds and insects and all living things that love light and freedom, rose to his feet. For as long as a man could hold his breath, Tane stood silent and unmoving, gathering his strength. He stood on his head with feet planted firmly against the Sky-father, and his hands pressed against the Earth. Then Tane straightened his back and thrust strongly against the Sky. A low moaning filled the air. It crept through the gods as they lay on the earth, for the sound trembled through the body of the Earth-mother when she felt Rangi's arms losing their hold upon her. The moaning grew louder until it became a roar. Rangi was hurled far away from Papa, and the angry winds screamed through the space that had opened between earth and sky.

Tane and his brothers looked round on the soft curves of their mother. For the first time they saw her in all her beauty, for the light had crept across the land. A silver veil of mist hung over Papa's naked shoulders and the tears that dropped fast from the eyes of Rangi were the sign that he grieved for her.

The gods breathed the free air and planned their new world. Although he had separated his parents, Tane loved them both, and he set to work to clothe his mother in beauty that had not been dreamed of in the dark world. He brought the trees, which were his own children, and set them in the earth; but because the world was still in the making and Tane was like a child learning by himself the wisdom that had not been born, he made mistakes and planted the trees with their heads in the soil with the bare white roots stiff and unmoving in the breeze.

Tane straightened his back and Rangi
was hurled far away from Papa.

He rested against the bole of a tree and frowned at his strange forest. It was no place for the birds and the insects, who are the merry children of Tane. He pushed over a giant kauri and set the roots firmly in the soil. Then he looked with pride at its lovely crown of leaves set above the clean, straight trunk. The rustling of the leaves was music in his ears.

The earth looked beautiful in her mantle of green. The brown-skinned men and women had come from their hiding places to frolic under the leaves of the garden of Tane. They lived in peace with Rongo-ma-tane and Haumia-tiketike. Tane-mahuta raised his eyes to where Rangi lay, cold and grey and unlovely in the vast spaces above the earth. He wept as he looked on the desolation of his father. Then he took the red sun and placed it at the back of Rangi, with the silver moon at the front. Up and down the ten heavens went Tane, till at length he found a wonderful garment of glowing red, which he took with him. He rested seven days after his mighty labours, and then he spread the red cloak over the heaven, from north to south, from east to west, so that Rangi glowed brightly. But he was not satisfied. The garment was not worthy of his father. He stripped it off, leaving only a little at the end of heaven, where you may see it at the time of the setting sun.

By day Rangi was good to look upon, and Papa watched her husband with pride, but at night Rangi lay dark and shapeless until Marama, the moon, shone upon him.

"Great father," cried Tane, "in the long, dark nights, before Marama shines on your breast, all things sorrow. I will journey to the end of space, my father, that I may find adornment for you." Somewhere in the silence far above, Tane heard an answering sigh.

Tane remembered the Shining Ones who play in the Great Mountain at the very end of all things. He passed swiftly to the end of the world, out into the unknown where the smiling face of earth could be seen no more; out into the darkness until he reached Maunganui, the Great Mountain, where the Shining Ones, the children of his brother Uru, lived. Tane greeted his brother and together they watched the Shining Ones playing on the sand far below at the foot of the mountain.

Uru listened as Tane told him how Rangi and Papa had been separated, and how he had come to beg from his brother some of the Shining Lights to fasten to the mantle of the sky. Uru rose to his feet and shouted so that the sound of his voice rolled like thunder down the mountain slopes. The Shining Ones heard. They stopped their game and came romping up the mountain to Uru. As they came nearer, Tane could see them rolling over and over, for every Shining One was shaped like an eye – an eye that glowed and twinkled, lighting up the whole mountain.

Uru placed a basket before Tane, and they plunged their arms into the glowing mass of lights and piled the Shining Ones into the basket. Tane picked it up and went swiftly towards his father. He placed four sacred lights in the four corners of the sky; five glowing lights he arranged in a cross on the breast of Rangi; the tiny Children of Light he fastened on to his father's robe.

The basket hangs in the wide heavens where we can see its soft light – the light which we call the Milky Way. It is this light that shelters the Shining Ones and protects the Children of Light. When the sun sank to rest, the stars twinkled brightly and Tane lay on his back and watched his father shake out his robe till the heavens were filled with the beauty of Rangi and the glory of the Shining Ones.

While Tane and those of his brothers who had clung to Mother Earth were happy in their new-found freedom, black-browed Tawhiri-matea held the winds in the hollow of his hand and bided his time. He saw Tane wandering idly in the forest. Far out at sea he saw his brother, Tangaroa, who lived at peace with his grand-children, Ika-tere, the father of fish, and Tu-te-wehiwehi, the father of reptiles. He rose and towered like a heavy black cloud over the distant sea and land. He opened his hand and hurled the winds across the empty spaces, and swept down from beneath his father's robes, wrapped in dark storm clouds and flashing lightning. He rushed over the land. The trees bent as the first winds reached them. Then came Tawhiri-matea and the tempest. The trees were uprooted, and when the wind died down the forest lay in tangled desolation.

The storm-god swept on to the brink of the ocean. The water boiled and surged in sudden fright. The waves rose until the sea seemed to empty itself and dissolve in the storm of flying spray and tempest-wrack. The empty sea-bottom appeared in the gaping valleys between the waves, and Tangaroa and his grandchildren fled down the valleys of their under-sea kingdom.

Tu-te-wehiwehi cried: "Let us fly to the shelter of the forest," but Ika-tere replied: "The sea is our only hope amidst the anger of the gods." So were the children of the children's children of Tangaroa divided. Tu-te-wehiwehi fled with the reptiles to the land, while Ika-tere hid his children in the sea. As they parted their voices rose above the screaming of Tawhiri-matea.

"Fly inland," shouted Ika-tere. "Fly inland then; but when you are caught, before you are cooked for food, they will singe off your scales with burning bracken."

"And as for you," cried Tu-te-wehiwehi, "who run away to the sea, your turn will come. When the little baskets of vegetables are given to the hungry ones, you will be laid on top to give relish to the food."

And so unending strife was caused by Tawhiri-matea, for Tangaroa never forgave his children who fled to Tane of the dry land. When the winds roar, Tangaroa hurls his waves against the land and tries to break down the beautiful realm of Tane and cover it with the cruel waves of the sea; but when the wind has blown itself out and the waters are calm, the sons and daughters of Tane creep out in their boats and snare the children of Tangaroa, that they may be used as relish in the vegetable baskets of the children of men.

Tawhiri's anger had not died down. He rushed upon Tu-matauenga, leaving a trail of destruction behind him. The sea roared sullenly and the forest giants lay broken amongst the tangled undergrowth, but Tu-matauenga held himself erect and did not bend before the fierce blasts. Tawhiri called all his winds to help him, but Tu defied him until at last Tawhiri went back to the Sky-father, defeated by the father of man.

Tu looked at the broken forests and the beaten sea.. "I am the conqueror of all," he said proudly. "My children shall never fear the children of the wind; the sons of Tane shall be their subjects; the sea will obey them as they ride the waves in the canoes that Tane will give them; fish and bird and root and berry shall be their food. I am Tu!"

And for this reason the sons of Tu-matauenga are lords of the forest and sea.

Tawhiri called all his winds to help him
but Tu defied him.

The swift days passed by at the bidding of the sun while Tane fashioned the birds and sent them gliding down the wind, until the air was filled with the song of the feathered ones. This was the manner of their creation, but as yet they did not know where to find food. Tane called them to him and told them to fly to Tutu and Karaka, and many others, to feed among their hair. The birds flew off and there they found rich berries, for Tutu and Karaka were trees, and amongst the forest foliage the birds still find insects and berries and honey which Tane has appointed for their food.

The world grew older and the little feathered children of Tane grew in number. Some went down to the sea and played in the great waters, or on the wet shining sands where land and water meet; but most of them went inland among the bright lights and cool shadows of the trees, where their voices made the forest ring with music. Some came out only at night and crept through the gloom while the others slept. Each bird knew its home and its time for going out and coming in, its song to sing and its food to eat – everyone, until boasting Kawau, the river cormorant, visited his cousin the sea cormorant. Kawau of the river was given a fish to eat, but as it slipped down, the spines caught in his gullet.

"Ah!" said Kawau, "you must come to my hunting place and I will show you eels that have no spines. In my kingdom I have fish a thousand times better than yours." He took his cousin with him, and when the sea cormorant caught an eel and found that Kawau's words were true, he begged that he might share the river kingdom with him. When Kawau of the river saw how quickly the eel slipped down his cousin's throat, he was sorry that he had boasted so loudly, and drove him away. The sea cormorant went quickly, but he spread the news of the wonderful spineless fish that swam in the fresh water of the rivers. The sea birds gathered themselves into a mighty array and flew inland to attack the land birds. On the morning of the battle, Pitoitoi the robin called out his warning and the land birds gathered together.

"Who'll be the scout?" asked Kawau. "Who'll see when they are coming?"

"I'll be the scout," said Koekoea the cuckoo, "I'll see when they are coming." Presently Koekoea saw a cloud of birds flying in from the sea.

Out of the warm red earth
Tane made a living woman.

"*Koo-o-o-e!*" The birds heard his cry, and a distant "*A-ha!*" as Karore the gull called back his challenge.

"Who'll answer their battle-cry?" asked Kawau.

"I," said the fantail. "With my fluttering tail I'll flaunt a challenge."

"Who'll lead the battle-song?" asked Kawau.

"I," said the tui. "Let Hongi the crow and Tirauke the saddle-back, and Wharauroa the short-tailed cuckoo, and Kuku the pigeon help me, and I'll lead the battle-song."

When their song was ended, Kawau faced the angry birds.

"Who'll begin the fight?" he cried.

"I'll begin the fight," shouted Ruru the owl. "With my beak and claws I'll begin the fight." He rose from his perch and swooped down on the sea birds, with the land birds flying in a great cloud behind him. Fierce was the battle, when feathers fell like snowflakes as the sun rose high in the heavens.

At last the sea birds grew fearful. The land birds attacked yet more fiercely until the ranks of the sea birds wavered and broke, and they turned tail and flew to their homes. The mocking laughter of the grey duck rang in their ears as they flew. "*Ke-ke-ke-ke!*" laughed Parera the duck as the gulls streamed out like a cloud unravelling in the wind.

No longer does the sea bird eat the land bird's food and there is peace between them in the world that great Tane-mahuta made with his hands when Rangi and Papa were separated and the light came in.

Tane had seen the beauty of earth and sky, but he was still dissatisfied. He felt that his work would be ended only when Papa was peopled with men and women. Children had been born to Tane and his brothers but they were celestial, never-dying gods who were not suited to earth and its ways.

The gods came down to earth and out of the warm red soil they made the image of a woman. She was lovely to look at, with soft skin and rounded form and long dark hair, but she was cold and lifeless. Then Tane bent down and breathed into her nostrils. Her eyelids fluttered and opened, and she looked round at the gods who were staring at her so intently. Then she sneezed. The breath of Tane had entered into her and she was a living woman.

The gods purified her and named her Hine-ahu-one, woman-created-from-earth. Tane became her husband and they had several girls as their children.

Tiki, the first man, was made by Tu-matauenga, god of war. He became the father of men and women who peopled the earth and inherited all the wonder and glory that Tane had made for them.

2

The Battle of
the Fishes

The tears ran down the woman's cheeks as she sat alone in her whare. Her husband had left her and she did not know where he had gone. She had asked the trees, but they were silent. The stream was enchanted and would give her no answer. The walls of the whare would not tell her. Only the calabash from which she drank took pity on her. As she lifted it to her lips, it spoke: "Do not grieve," it said. "Break me on the floor, gather up the fragments and take me with you. I will show you the way he went."

The woman thanked the calabash. Dashing it on the floor, she picked up the pieces, put them in a basket of flax, and set out. The broken calabash told her the path to follow. She went on till she reached the bank of the enchanted stream. As she waded through it the water crept into the basket, and when she reached the further shore the calabash was dumb once more.

The woman returned to her whare sorrowfully, for there were scores of paths under the trees and she could not tell which one to follow. In the dark night her heart was filled with bitterness because her husband had left her. She heard the booming of the ocean waves on the shore and decided to ask Tangaroa, god of the sea, for his help to avenge the wrong that had been done to her. Like a wild creature of the woods she slipped between the trees till she came to the pale sand. With her face lifted to the stars and arms outstretched, she cried aloud:

"Hear my prayer, ruler of the sea. Great wrong has been done to me by my husband, and by men who have hidden him from me. Comfort me by destroying these evil ones."

Tangaroa needed little encouragement to make war on the subjects of his brother of the land. In a voice like thunder he called

The palisades of the pa cracked and splintered
at the whales' onslaught.

to his people, the fishes. They came to him quickly. Great and small, every one was there, and all alike, for they wore the grey livery of the children of Ika-tere, and they were all of the same shape. Only in size did they differ, from Tohora the whale down to Inanga the whitebait. Like a mighty army they swam to the shore, to the village where the errant husband was living.

In the vanguard was the tribe of the gurnards, and the rear was brought up by the whales whose huge bodies would act as a bulwark to stem the rush if the smaller fish fled at the onslaught of the Maoris. They reached the shore and climbed out on to the sand. They crashed through the undergrowth of the forest lands. Their wet shining bodies lumbered on, and presently they heard a wild cry of alarm as their dim grey shapes were seen under the trees.

All day long that dreadful battle raged. The gurnards stormed the palisades of the pa, and many of them were killed, so that they were dyed red with their own blood, even as they are to this day. Parore the black perch followed close in support of the gurnard, until his warriors were covered with the dried blood of the advance guard.

Tribe after tribe, they hurled themselves into the fray. As the sun slid down the western sky they saw the dead bodies of their comrades all around them, and the little fishes were frightened. They turned back and fled into the cool shadows of the protecting bush where Tohora and his great warriors lay in reserve.

When he saw the little fishes retreating in panic, he bellowed out his orders. The whales lurched forward. The trees tossed like raupo leaves in the wind as they pushed between them. The palisades of the pa cracked and splintered at their onslaught; they fell with crashes that shook the ground.

The defenders of the pa fled in sudden terror, and victory was won. The dwellers of the sea had defeated the tangata whenua, the people of the land.

The next day Tangaroa stood in his ocean home. His victorious army swam round him in a great circle, and as each tribe passed the god, he gave it the boon that was asked.

The gurnards wore the honourable badge of their faithfulness, the rich red blood of the fishes who had led the hosts of war.

Patiki the flounder had seen a boy's toy and wished to be shaped like a kite.

Takeke the garfish proudly bore a spear under his fin and asked that he might wear it in his head.

Whai, the stingray, too had a spear, one with a double row of barbs at its point, and this he wanted at the end of his tail.

Last of all came Araara the trevally, bearing a white cape that he had taken from the man who had left his wife. The cape was mottled with bright red stains of blood, and this became the garment of the trevally.

So did Tangaroa avenge the wrong that had been done, and gave to the fishes their wonderful shapes and colours. The children of Ika-tere to this day wear the proud scars and the insignia of war that they had gained on the day they defeated Man.

3

Mataora and Niwareka in the Underworld

In the days of long ago, Mataora, the warrior chief, tossed restlessly in his sleep. He dreamed that his taiaha was in his hand, and that he was engaged in a combat to the death. All round him were men and women seated on the ground, crying out in delight at every thrust and blow. Then in his dream the cries of the people changed to laughter. He looked round in amazement. The clouds of sleep drifted away from his eyes and he sprang to his feet. White faces were peering at him through the doorway and the window. He looked round and saw the flame of their hair framed in the opening like the plume of the toetoe in the morning sun.

"Who are you?" he cried.

"We are the Turehu," came the reply.

"Where do you come from?"

"We come from the Underworld. What are you? Are you a god?" one of them asked. Another said: "Are you a man?" and at this they laughed, for the Turehu were all women.

"Why do you ask?" Mataora said angrily. "Can you not see that I am a man?"

They laughed again. "We did not know because you are not tattooed. The designs are only painted on your face."

He stared at them in surprise. "How else could they be drawn?" he asked.

No one answered for a moment, but presently a tall girl said: "Some day perhaps you will know."

Mataora forgot her reply at once. He was filled with curiosity, for the Turehu had never been seen in that place before. "Come inside," he invited, "and I will give you something to eat."

"Yes, we will eat," they said, "but we will wait outside."

Mataora hurried to his storehouse and brought cooked food. The Turehu were strange in their ways. "Is it good?" they asked, and someone who had looked at it said: "No, it is bad."

Mataora was angry when he heard this. "Look," he shouted, "I will show you," and he ate some himself. The Turehu crowded round him, smiling and nodding to themselves as they watched him. One of them opened his mouth and looked inside and cried: "Oh, he has eaten mussels!" while several others shouted, "It is bad food!"

When they said this Mataora remembered hearing that the Turehu ate their food raw, so he went to the pond and caught them some fish and put them in front of the fair-skinned women.

The Turehu laughed again with delight and quickly finished them up. While they were eating Mataora watched them closely. They had fair skins and flaxen hair which grew to their waists. They held themselves erect and their noses were thin. They wore waistmats of dried seaweed.

When they had finished their meal, Mataora sprang to his feet and danced before them. As he whirled round he noticed one young woman watching him closely. She was taller than the others and Mataora could pick her out at once from her companions. Every time their eyes met he felt love for her rising inside him.

He sat down, and the Turehu joined together in a stately dance. It was different from any poi-dance or haka that Mataora had ever seen. The tall girl who had been watching him came to the front and wove a pattern with her feet. The others joined hands and followed her, bending under their companions' arms and gliding in and out till Mataora grew dizzy watching them. They sang as they danced but the only words he could hear were:

> *Here goes Niwareka,*
> *Niwareka, Niwareka.*

When the dance was over, Mataora asked them if he could choose a wife from amongst them.

"Which of us do you want?" they asked, crowding eagerly towards him.

He pointed to the tall girl who was behind her friends. There was more laughter and jostling until the young woman came forward shyly and pressed noses with Mataora. As he held her hand he felt contentment in his heart. Presently the Turehu went away, while Mataora and his wife stood at the door watching them.

"Where are they going now?" he asked, and Niwareka replied a little sadly, "Back to the Underworld, where everything is beautiful and full of light."

Mataora put his arm round her. "Ah, no, you will find the light only where Te Ra, the hot sun, shows himself. Tell me, my wife, who is your father?"

She turned to him. "I am called Niwareka. I am the daughter of high-born Ue-tonga of Rarohenga, the Underworld, but now I belong to Mataora; the mighty chieftain of the Overworld.

Mataora loved his wife dearly, and the passing days increased that love. There was only one thing that ever caused a dark cloud to rise in their sky. Mataora sometimes had moods and fits of evil temper, and in one of these he struck his wife. She looked at him sorrowfully, for the Turehu are gentle people, and not used to violence.

That night Niwareka ran away from home, and though Mataora searched everywhere for her, he could not find her. He missed her and sorrowed, for the light had gone out of his life. When many days had passed and she had not returned, he knew that she had gone back to her home in Rarohenga, the Underworld. He determined to follow her, even though he knew the dangers of the journey that lay ahead.

Presently he came to the House of the Four Winds where the spirits of the dead return to Rarohenga. He asked the guardian of the House: "Have you seen a woman pass this way?"

"What is she like?" was the reply.

"She is beautiful and pale, with long flaxen hair and fair skin, and a straight nose."

The guardian said: "Ah, yes, I have seen her. She passed this way many days ago, weeping as she went."

"May I follow her?"

"Yes," said the guardian, "you may follow if you have the courage. This is the way."

He opened a door and through it Mataora saw a tunnel leading downwards. He lowered himself into it and the door was shut behind him. There was no glimmer of light anywhere and the place felt airless and cold. He felt his way down through the thick darkness until, after hours of stumbling and silence, he saw a light shining in the distance. He hurried on, and soon in the half-light he saw Tiwaiwaka the fantail fluttering about.

"Have you seen a woman pass this way?" Mataora asked.

Tiwaiwaka said: "Yes, I have seen her. Her eyes were red with weeping."

Mataora quickened his steps until he came to the end of the tunnel. He came out into a new world. There was no sun, nor any blue in the sky above. Only the rocks roofed the vast world he had entered, but light seemed to fill every part of it; birds sang and reeds and grasses waved in the breeze, and somewhere he could hear water moving over stones. He went on till he came to the village where Ue-tonga, the father of Niwareka, lived.

Ue-tonga was sitting on the ground and Mataora stopped to watch him. A young man was stretched full length on the ground while Ue-tonga cut lines into his face with a bone chisel and hammer, and smeared pigment into the wounds. Mataora looked on in astonishment as he saw blood flowing under the sharp edge of the chisel.

"That is not the way to tattoo!" he cried. "Up above we paint the designs in red and white and blue."

Ue-tonga looked up at him. "Bend down your head," he ordered.

Mataora bent his head and Ue-tonga rubbed his hand quickly across his face. The painted design was wiped off, and he heard the laughter of the fair-haired people that had woken him from his dream when he first met Niwareka. He looked round to see if there was one woman taller than the rest, but he could not recognise anyone he knew.

"You see how useless your painted moko is," Ue-tonga said. "You have not learned the art. Here in Rarohenga we carve designs in the flesh so that they will never wear out."

Mataora looked closely at Ue-tonga's face and saw ridges and grooves there, stained with the pigment that remains fast through the changing years. When he saw the whorls that had come from the hand of a master-craftsman, he felt ashamed of the simple design that had been painted on his face.

"You have destroyed my moko," he said to Ue-tonga. "Now you must carve it on me."

"It is well," said Ue-tonga simply. "Lie down."

Mataora lay on his back while the design was drawn on his face with charcoal. Ue-tonga bent over him and tapped the bone chisel into his flesh. Mataora shuddered as he felt the rending edge. A tuft of grass that was caught in his hand snapped at the roots. The tap-tapping chisel crept slowly across his face while waves of agony swept over his body. Presently he began to sing:

> Niwareka, where are you?
> Show yourself, O Niwareka!
> 'Tis love of you that brought me here,
> Niwareka, Niwareka.

The younger sister of Niwareka was not far away. She heard the words of his song and hurried to her sister. "A man is being tattooed over there and he keeps calling your name. Who can it be?"

Niwareka's friends said: "Let us all go and see."

They crowded over to the place of tattooing. Ue-tonga was annoyed at the interruption. "What do you want here?" he called.

Niwareka replied: "We have come to fetch the stranger to the village to entertain him."

By this time Ue-tonga had finished, for the operation was painful and he could see that Mataora could bear no more. The brown-skinned man got slowly to his feet. His face was swollen and disfigured and streaming with blood, so that no one recognised him, but there were many exclamations at his broad shoulders and handsome figure. Niwareka watched him closely. "This is the body of Mataora," she said, "and these are the garments I wove for him."

When he had sat down, she stood at a little distance from him and said: "Are you Mataora?"

He could not see her, for his eyes were sunken in his swollen face, but as soon as she spoke, Mataora knew her voice. He beckoned with his hand and she knew that he was indeed her husband, and came and wept over him for joy.

When the tattooing was finished and the wounds had healed,

Ue-tonga bent over Mataora and tapped
the bone chisel into his flesh.

Mataora said to Niwareka: "Let us know return to our longstanding world above Rarohenga."

Niwareka looked at him. "I think we should stay here," she said. "Let us ask my father."

Ue-tonga said at once: "Let it be you alone who goes back, Mataora. Niwareka will stay here." He looked straight at his son-by-marriage. "I have heard it said that men sometimes beat their wives in the Upper World."

Mataora was ashamed. "That is past," he replied. "In future I will follow only the good that is done in Rarohenga."

Ue-tonga smiled. "If your words come from the heart, my son, you may go and take Niwareka with you. The Upper World is a place of darkness, but here in Rarohenga it is full of light. Take our light into your world of darkness."

"Look at my face," said Mataora. "Now you have carved it with the moko of the Lower World, and it will never wash off. So is my desire to follow the ways of peace and love."

The reunited husband and wife set off together. When they came to the entrance of the tunnel that leads to the Upper World they were met by Tiwaiwaka.

"You will need someone to guide you," he said. "Take Popoia and Peka with you."

"If we take them they will be chased by the forest birds of Tane."

"They will hide in the darkness of the night," said Tiwaiwaka. So they took the owl and the bat with them to become birds of the night, and these two showed them the way through the tunnel.

At last they came to the House of the Four Winds, and the guardian said to Niwareka: "What is in the bundle you are carrying?"

She replied: "It is nothing. It is only the clothes we must wear in the Upper World."

The guardian frowned. "It is more than that. You are trying to deceive me. I will never allow anyone to come again from Rarohenga to the Upper World. The way is closed. Only the spirits of the dead may pass on their way to Rarohenga. You have there the garment of Te Rangihaupapa."

"It is so," Niwareka admitted, for she had brought it to the

Upper World as a pattern for the beautiful borders that women wore on their cloaks in after years.

The guardian held out his hand and Niwareka placed the bundle in it. The guardian unrolled it. Its colours shone in that gloomy place when he hung it on one of the walls.

Mataora and Niwareka passed on as his back was turned. They went to their own home, and there they lived happily for the rest of their days.

It was Mataora who handed on to men the secret of the moko that cannot be rubbed off; and it was Niwareka who taught women how to weave coloured borders for their cloaks. From their love came these things, from the love of Mataora and Niwareka in the beginning of the world.

4

Maui the Half-God

Far out in mid-ocean a bundle of seaweed rose and fell on the waves. Overhead the seabirds wheeled and screamed. A baby, tightly wrapped in its mother's hair, lay cradled in the seaweed that protected it from the birds and the terrors of the deep water. The baby was Maui, little Maui wrapped in the top-knot of his mother, Taranga. It was Maui, the fifth son, the unwanted, who had been thrown into the sea, with only his mother's hair to cover him.

Presently the bundle was washed ashore and as it lay on the sand, the birds became bolder and the flies clustered round it. The baby began to cry, for the seaweed was shrivelling and falling away, and the flies were beginning to settle on its tender skin. From his house by the cliffs, great Tama of heaven heard the thin wailing cry. He ran to the heap of seaweed, lifted the tangled hair, and unwrapped the baby. His eyes widened as he saw little Maui lying there, blue with cold. Holding the baby very carefully, he hurried with it to the house and tied it to the rafters where it swung gently to and fro in the warmth from the fire, and presently began to laugh and wave its arms.

This was Maui's first adventure, in which he was saved from death by the friendly seaweed, and the old man who lived on the borders of the sky. As he grew up, he learned many things from wise old Tama; the ways of the birds and their language, and of the cunning of fish; the games that are played by children and the thoughts of the old people as they sit round the fire at night. He grew in height, and learned about the forest creatures, and magic that made them his friends. Last of all he learned where his mother lived.

"Now I go to my own people," he said to Tama one day.

"Yes, you will go to your own people," Tama replied sadly. "You will leave the old man who has taught you so much. You will do

Tama's eyes widened as he saw
little Maui there, blue with cold.

many wonderful things, Maui, and there is only one who will be
able to stop you. You will have many adventures, but the last will
be the greatest of all, and you will lose in that fight. No, my son, I
will not tell you what it is. It will be a good thing to be in that fight,
but it will not matter that you lose. We all lose that fight, Maui, but
you will not be forgotten. Now go quickly, my son; the world is
waiting for you."

Maui ran along the sand dunes. He climbed the hills to the west
and dropped down on to the plains. In the distance there was a
house with a thin curl of smoke rising above it. In his bones he felt
that this was his mother's whare. It was dark by the time he reached
it, but he was guided through the forest by the sound of singing. He
looked round the door and saw that a fire was burning on the floor
and that the smoke was rolling through the house. Maui slipped
inside like a shadow and sat down behind one of his brothers
without being seen. Presently his mother came up to her children
and said, "Stand up when I call you, so that we may dance. Maui-
taha!"

The eldest brother stood up.

"That's one. Maui-roto! That's two, Maui-pae! That's three.
Maui-waho! That's four. All my sons are ready.

Then little Maui stood up and came out of the shadows. "I am
Maui, too," he said.

His mother stared at him. "Oh no, you are not Maui. All my
sons are here. I counted them myself!"

"I am Maui," the boy insisted. "These are my brothers. See, I
know their names: Maui-taha, you, Maui-roto, Maui-pae and Maui-
waho. Now I have come, and I am Maui the little one."

"I have never seen you before," his mother replied, while Maui-
taha, Maui-roto, Maui-pae and Maui-waho stared at their brother.
"No, you cannot be Maui, little stranger. Where do you come from?"

"I come from the sea. The waves were my cradle, the fish and
birds fought for me, but I was wrapped in my mother's hair."

His mother caught up a torch and held it close to his face.

"What is my name?" she asked suddenly.

"You are my mother, Taranga."

She leaned forward then and clasped him to her. "Yes, you are
indeed my little Maui," she said. "I have found you again. You will

be the fifth Maui, and your name will be Maui-tikitiki-a-Taranga – Maui who was wrapped in the topknot of Taranga. You will live here with your brothers and you will be my own little son again."

Maui-tikitiki-a-Taranga was a mischief, and now he had four brothers to torment. When they played with their kites, little Maui's always flew the highest. When they played tag, which they called wi, Maui always ran the fastest. When darts were thrown, Maui's fern frond always went the furthest. At the breath-holding game, Maui could always recite the longest. At swimming and diving, Maui was always boldest. He was a friend of all the forest folk, and because of the magic he had learned from Tama, he could turn himself into a bird and escape from his brothers when they were angry with him.

Because he could do all these things, and poke fun at them for being dull and slow, his brothers hated him. But Maui did not mind that, for he laughed at them and went off to play with his friends the birds. Only one thing ever made him unhappy. He had never seen his father. Every night he slept beside his mother on the floor of the whare, but when he woke in the morning, she was not there, and he did not see her again until night came.

"Where does my mother go in the daytime?" he asked his brothers.

"How should we know?" they said.

"Because you have known her longer than I."

"She may go north or south, east or west. We do not care," they said.

When Maui saw that they would not tell him, he made up his mind to find out for himself.

One night he stayed awake, and when he heard his mother breathing softly and knew that she was asleep, he crept to her and, taking her beautiful girdle and apron, he hid them under his sleeping mat. Then he went to every window in the house and blocked up the cracks where the light would creep in when morning came.

At daybreak, Maui's mother woke up and raised herself to see whether it was light. Outside the clouds were tinged with pink, but in the whare there was not even a glimmer of light. She lay back and went to sleep. When she woke up again, the inside of the whare was still dark, but the birds were singing. Taranga sprang to her feet and opened the windows, and saw the golden sunlight everywhere. She looked for her girdle and apron, but they were not there, so without waiting to search for them, she threw an old cloak round her shoulders and ran outside.

The sudden light in the whare wakened Maui, and he slipped after his mother and followed her outside. Presently he saw her stoop and pull up a tussock of grass. Underneath there was a big hole into which Taranga dropped lightly, pulling the grass back over it again.

Maui knew now that his mother spent her days in the twilit underworld. He hurried back to his brothers.

"I have found where our mother goes during the hours of daylight," he cried. "She goes to our father in the shadow land. Let us follow her, my brothers."

"Why should we care where she goes?" one of them said and the others agreed. "Yes, what do we care? Rangi, the Great Heaven, is our father, and Papa, the Earth, is our mother."

"Then I shall find her," Maui said. "She is my mother. She brings us food and stays with us at night and loves us. I will find her."

He took his mother's girdle and her cloak, and dressed himself in them. While his brothers watched, Maui shrank to a tenth of his size, and they saw a beautiful pigeon where he had been standing. The girdle shone white and pure on his breast, and the soft glowing colours of his feathers were taken from his mother's apron. The brothers cried out in delight as he lifted his wings and soared over the trees to the place where his mother had disappeared. A moment later he had lifted the tuft of grass and plunged into the hole underneath.

He dipped his wings where the cave was narrow and flew on through the winding passages that lead to the underworld, until he came at length to a fair land where there was no sun, and the air was still. There were trees growing in that place, tall and leafy, but there was no breath of wind to stir the leaves. He flew on to a low branch and perched there.

Presently several men and women passed by. Two of them stopped and sat down under the tree where Maui had perched. One was his mother, and Maui knew that the man must be his father. He picked a berry with his beak and dropped it so that it fell on his

Maui's father threw a stone and the pigeon
fluttered down to his feet.

father's head. His mother said, "The berry must have been dropped by a bird."

"No," said his father, "it was ripe and its time for falling had come."

Then Maui picked a cluster of berries and threw them so that they hit both his mother and father. They sprang to their feet, while other people came hurrying up, for they too had seen the pigeon. The birds of the underworld were drab and grey. The men threw stones at the beautiful bird, trying to dislodge it from its perch. Maui shifted from side to side, and dodged the stones.

At last Maui's father threw a stone, and the pigeon at once tumbled off the perch and fluttered down to his feet. It grew bigger, it lost the shape of a bird, it grew tall and slender, and there stood a young man, with the beautiful cloak round his shoulders and the white girdle shining against his brown skin.

Maui's mother knew her son. "It is not Maui-taha, my first-born," she said, "nor Maui-roto, the second, nor Maui-pae, the third, nor yet Maui-waho. It is my little Maui, my youngest son, Maui-tikitiki-a-Taranga," and she held him tightly to her. "This is the child who came by wind and wave. You will bring joy and sorrow to the world, you will bind the sun, Maui, maybe you will conquer even Death herself."

Maui went with his father to be baptised, and the spells that were repeated over him helped to make him brave, and unconquerable to the last.

So Maui, the littlest one, lived happily with his parents, and the pigeons that flitted through the bush were glad, because they now wore the glowing colours of the cloak of Maui's mother.

But Make-tu-tara, the father of Maui, and Taranga, the mother of Maui, were sad, for they knew that part of the spell had been forgotten at his baptism, and Maui could never hope to conquer the goddess of death in his last and greatest deed.

As he grew familiar with the underworld, Maui noticed that food was prepared carefully each day, and taken to someone whose name was never spoken. Maui liked to know the reason for everything, so he asked, "Who is that food for?"

"It is for your grandfather, Muri-ranga-whenua."

"Ah, I have heard of him," Maui said. "Let me take the food to him."

He took the basket and carried it off to the gloomy home where Muri lived; but instead of taking it to the old man, he laid it down in a dark place where no one could see it. Each day Maui took the food and hid it, until Muri became hungry. His voice rumbled through the arched caverns, "Where is my food? Who is robbing me?"

Maui stood still while his grandfather sniffed the food. "If I catch him, I will eat him," the old man cried. He turned and sniffed the south wind, but he could not smell anything. He turned to the north, but there was no man-scent there. He turned to the east, but again there was no smell. Lastly he turned to the west, and sniffed.

"Aha," he cried, "I smell him. What does a silent man-thing in the lonely underworld?" He sniffed again. "Is it Maui, my grandson, the little one?" he called.

"Yes, it is I, Maui-tikitiki-a-Taranga."

"Why are you taking my food, little Maui?" What do you want, little Maui?"

"I want your jawbone, Muri my grandfather," Maui replied. "Give my your jawbone, and I will give you food, and leave you in peace."

Muri thought for a while. "Bring the food, Maui," came the deep rumbling voice again. "Bring all the food. I am old and have no need of my jawbone. Take it, for you will need it soon."

Maui went forward fearlessly. He took the sacred jawbone of Muri and hurried back to his mother's home. He hid it under his mat, and treasured it until the time came when he could use it.

Maui grew up and became a man. He married a woman of the upper world and went to live in the village with his brothers. Each day the sun god rose with a bound and travelled quickly across the sky. While light remained, the morning meal was hastily prepared and eaten, and then in a little while it was dark again. The people grumbled because the hours of sunlight were so short, but no one ever thought of trying to alter them. Only Maui watched the sun hurrying across the sky, and thought about it, until at last he knew what could be done.

"The days are too short," he said to his brothers.

"Yes, they are not long enough for us to do our work. That is why our games are always played in the dark," they said.

"We must make them longer," Maui declared.

His brothers laughed. "Is the sun a bird, to be caught while it perches on a branch?" they asked.

"Yes," Maui replied seriously. "I will snare it like a sitting bird."

His brothers laughed louder. "Are you a god to think that you can face the sun god in his strength?"

Maui's eyes blazed. "You forget my power too soon, my brothers. Can I not change myself into a bird? Am I not the strongest of all men? Whose is the magic jawbone of Muri our grandfather? Tomorrow we will journey towards the rising of the sun, and there we will make a snare of strong rope and catch him and tame him."

"But the ropes will burn. He will break them like single threads, and we shall shrivel up in the heat of his anger," they objected.

"Get your wives to bring flax and we will make the rope now," Maui said firmly, and because of the fire in his eyes, and because they were afraid of him, Maui's brothers sat down and plaited a strong rope. Then Maui took the magic jawbone and, followed by his brothers carrying the rope, he set out towards the place of the rising sun. They hid in the daytime, but at night they travelled fast, until at last they reached the edge of the world. There they built a long clay wall behind which they could hide and shelter themselves from the heat of the sun. They built houses made of branches at each end of the wall, and hid themselves in them, Maui in one and his brothers in the other. Above the place where the sun rose, they set a great rope noose and covered it with branches and green leaves.

Presently the sun rose in his strength. The brothers had the end of the rope in their hands. "Steady," whispered Maui. "Wait till his head and shoulders are through. A-a-h! Now!" The brothers pulled on the rope. Aha, they pulled the rope which had settled round the body of Tama the sun, till it quivered and sang the song of strong ropes that are stretched to breaking point. Tama felt the pain like a circle of fire round his body. He saw the wall and the huts made of branches, and the rope that stretched from his body to the door of the hut. In his anger he threw himself from side to side. He caught

The air rang with the cries
of the sun god.

the woven flax in his hands to snap it, but it was too strongly made. He pushed with his feet against the earth and the singing of the rope swelled like insects in the bush in summer. It slipped through the hands of the brothers, and the sound of their heavy breathing could be heard above the roaring of the sun.

Maui left his hut with his weapon in his hand, and ran along behind the shelter of the wall. He rose to his full height and brought Muri's bone down with all his strength on Tama's head. Again and again he struck, while the air rang with the cries of the sun god. His head fell forward, and Maui's brothers gathered up the slack of the rope. Maui's blows still felt like the noise of forest trees crashing to the ground when they are felled by fire. At length the sun god was beaten to his knees and cried for mercy.

Then they let him go, for he was badly wounded, and his strength had left him. Instead of leaping swiftly along the path from morning to night, he travelled slowly, as he does to this very day.

Maui's restless mind was never satisfied with the answers he received to his questions.

"Where does fire come from?" he wanted to know.

"It is here," the people replied impatiently. "Why do you want to know where it comes from? If it is ours, do we need to know how it comes to us?"

"But what happens if the fires go out?"

"We do not let them go out. If that should happen, our mother knows where to obtain the fire, but she will not tell us."

That night, when everyone was asleep, Maui left his whare and crept to the cooking fires that were smouldering in the darkness. Quietly he poured water on them until the last spark was quenched.

As soon as the sky flushed with the first rays of dawn, Maui called to his servants, "I am hungry. Cook some food quickly." They ran to the fires, only to find heaps of grey ash. There was an outcry in the village as the servants rushed to and fro with the news. Maui stayed in his whare and smiled to himself as he listened to the noise. Presently he heard the sound of voices on the marae, the village meeting-place. His mother was telling the slaves to go to the underworld to get more fire.

Maui threw his kiwi feather cloak round him and strode on to the marae. The slaves were huddled together in terror, for they dreaded the underworld. "I will go, my mother. Where shall I find the land of darkness? Who is the keeper of the fire?"

Taranga looked at her son suspiciously. "If no one will go, then my youngest son must make the journey. If you keep to the path that I will show you, you will come to the house of Mahuika, your ancestress. She is the guardian of the fire. If she asks your name, tell her who you are. You must be careful. Be respectful, my son. We know the ways of Maui-tikitiki-a-Taranga, but your ancestress is powerful, and if you try to deceive her, she will punish you."

Maui grinned mischievously and set off at once with a long, steady pace that covered the ground quickly, and soon took him to the shadowy land where the fire goddess lived. Presently he came to a beautiful whare with splendid carvings, with paua-shell eyes that shone like flame in the darkness. A woman's voice, old and broken, like the crackling of branches in the fire, came to his ears.

"Who is the bold mortal that stares at the whare of Mahuika of the Fire?"

"It is Maui."

"I have five grandchildren called Maui. Is it Maui-tikitiki-a-Taranga?"

"Yes, it is I."

The old woman chuckled. "What do you want from your grandmother, Maui-the-last-one?"

"I want fire to take back to my mother and my brothers."

"I can give you fire, Maui."

Mahuika pulled out one of her fingernails, and it burst into flame. "Carry it carefully, Maui, and light your fires with it."

Maui took it away, but when he had gone a little distance, he threw it on the ground and stamped on it until the fire was beaten out. He went back to the whare.

"Aha, it is Maui again," the old woman called. "What do you want this time, Maui?"

"Fire. I have lost it. The flame went out."

Mahuika scowled. "Then you have been careless, my grandchild. I will give you another fingernail, but you must shield the flame with your hand."

Mahuika pulled out one of her fingernails
and it burst into flame.

Maui took the burning fingernail. When he was out of sight, he beat out the flame and returned to Mahuika. The fire goddess scowled at him, and rumbled as she gave him another.

Five times Maui went away with the flame, and five times he returned empty-handed. Ten times he went away, and ten times he returned empty-handed. Mahuika's fingernails had all been given away. Grudgingly she gave him one of her toenails, but in a little while the crafty Maui came back for another. Five times he went away, and five times he returned empty-handed. Nine times he went away and nine times he returned empty-handed.

Then at last Mahuika's patience was exhausted. The subterranean fires shook the house, and Maui had to force his way through the heat and the smoke that poured from the door and window. Mahuika's eyes glared through the darkness like flashes of lightning. She took her toenail and threw it at Maui. It fell short, and as it touched the ground there was a noise like thunder, and a sheet of flame travelled with the speed of wind towards Maui. He ran as quickly as he could, but the flames were like a taniwha roaring after him. He changed to the form of a hawk and flew onwards with great strokes of his wings, but still the flames gained on him. He could feel the heat singeing his feathers, and to this day you will see that the plumage of the hawk remains brown where the fire touched it.

A pool of water lay before him, and folding his wings he plunged into it. Presently the water grew warm. Maui stirred uneasily at the bottom of the pool. It was beginning to get hot now. A few moments later it started to boil and Maui flew upward. The air was full of flame. The forest was on fire and the flames were spreading up into the sky.

It seemed as though the whole world was in danger of being destroyed by fire. Then Maui remembered the gods he had known in Tama's house. He called to them and they saw that the earth was in peril. They sent down rain, heavy driving rain that hurled itself against the flames, and flattened their crests, and broke through the walls of fire. A harsh voice was heard crying in terror. Mahuika was in the midst of the fire, and as she turned and fled to her home, her strength began to fail her. The flames subsided into fitful little tongues, and died suddenly in a puff of steam. Mahuika threw the last of her fire into the trees, and they gave it shelter and saved it for the children of men. These trees were kaikomako, the mahoe and the totara.

At the last, then, there came goodness from the mischief of Maui, for men learnt to rub the wood of these trees together so that fire came from them, and they could at any time summon the fire children of Mahuika to their aid.

Maui patted his fish-hook lovingly. It had been made from the jawbone of his grandfather Muri-ranga-whenua. It was inlaid with mother-of-pearl and ornamented with tufts of dog's hair, and deep magic lay under its polished surface.

The sun had not yet lifted itself above the sea when Maui crept from his whare and climbed into his brothers' canoe. He lifted the bottom boards and slipped into the cramped space underneath. Pulling the boards over himself again, he lay down.

He did not have long to wait. The eastern sky was still pink when the brothers of Maui piled their fishing-lines into the canoe and launched it into the breakers. Maui, hidden beneath their feet, heard them laughing together. "We have got rid of Maui, the tiny one," Maui-pae said. "He will still be asleep."

"Maui is not sleeping," said a deep voice. They looked round in amazement. It sounded as though it had come from beneath the canoe.

"Perhaps it is a gull," said Maui-waho, but they did not believe him.

They lifted their paddles again and the canoe sped forward. Then they stopped. This time there was no mistake. It was Maui who was laughing at them. They pulled up the boards and there he was, grinning at them like a goblin.

"Maui!" they cried. "We will not take you with us. You will spoil our fishing."

Maui's grin widened. "You will take me," he said.

"No. We will put back now. Our canoe is large enough for Maui-pae, for Maui-roto, for Maui-waho, for Maui-taha; it is too small for Maui-tikitiki-a-Taranga."

"You will take me," Maui repeated. He stretched out his arm and pointed towards the land. The brothers looked behind them,

but only the blue ocean of Kiwa was to be seen, for by his magic art
Maui had spread out the sea, and the land was lost behind the lift
of the waves.

"Paddle on," he commanded.

"No," said his brothers, laying down their paddles.

"Paddle on!" cried Maui. The laughter had faded from his face,
and his eyes were cold and hard like chips of greenstone. The four
brothers lifted their paddles and bent their backs.

They were weary when he gave the word to stop. "Let out your
lines," he said, "and we shall see what the fishing-ground of my
choice will yield."

They baited their hooks in silence and let them down into the
water. Soon the lines jerked in their hands, and before long the
bottom boards were covered with fish.

"That will do," said the eldest brother. "This has been good
fishing. Now it is done."

Maui breathed on his fish-hook and admired it as it caught the
light. "You have done your work, my brothers," he said softly.
"Mine has not yet begun."

"No, no," they cried at once. "We have enough for you as well
as for ourselves, Maui, Let us go home to our wives and children
now."

"Ah, my brothers, you have not seen the fishing of Maui. Only
once shall I let out my line. Give me some bait."

They would not give him any for they feared what their brother
might do. Then Maui clenched his fist and struck his nose so
violently that it bled. He smeared the blood on the hook and
lowered it over the side of the canoe.

Fathom after fathom of line passed between his fingers. The flax
cord stretched far into the depths. Presently Maui felt that the hook
had touched something. He breathed softly while his brothers
looked on in silence. He tugged gently at the cord, and far below
the hook caught fast.

In the silent home of Tangaroa, Maui's hook had caught in the
doorway of the house of Tonganui, the son of the sea god. Maui
took the strain on his line. He set his feet against the side of the
canoe, and putting forth his strength, he hauled on the line.
Tonganui's house groaned. It lifted a little, settled back and then, as

the quivering cord strained upwards, it left the bottom of the sea, and with it came a great piece of land.

Maui chanted the song that makes heavy weights light. His brothers drove their paddles deep in the water. Maui's voice rose higher, and his muscles stood out on his arms like the roots of a tree. The cord sang with a high head-piercing note.

There was a deep-throated cry from the brothers as the teko-teko, the carved human figure on the roof of Tonganui's house, rose slowly above the sea, followed by the sides and the doorway, with the magic hook caught in it. And then came the land underneath, like a shining fish whose tail stretched far out of sight. It lifted the canoe high out of the water as it thrust the ocean from its sides.

It was the Fish of Maui ... Te Ika a Maui.

"Remain here," said Maui to his brothers. "Make no sound. The sea god is angry, and I must make peace with him. Then we will divide the land between us."

He passed out of sight with long swinging strikes. Smooth and bright and shining was the world that Maui had pulled from beneath the sea. On its broad surface were houses. Fires were sending columns of smoke in the still air. Birds were singing, and streams were chattering down its sides.

"This piece belongs to me," shouted Maui-taha.

"No, it is mine," called Maui-waho.

"Well, then, I shall take this," said Maui-pae. They sprang out of the canoe and ran about the land, slashing it with their weapons, and claiming pieces for themselves.

The Fish felt their running feet and the strokes of their weapons. It was but sleeping on the surface of the ocean. It tossed on the water, and its smooth surface was ruffled.

That is why the Great Fish of Maui has been broken into mountain and valley, and rough and rocky coastlines. If they had left it alone it would be smooth to this very day.

It happened long ago, this fishing of Maui. Te Ika a Maui they called it, the Great Fish of Maui, this Northern Island of Aotearoa. Even the hook is here. It stretches out in the curved coastline of Hawke's Bay, to the point known to the Maori as Te Matau a Maui ... the Fishhook of Maui.

It was the fish of Maui
– Te Ika a Maui.

Tuna-roa was the father of all eels. He lived in a swamp on the back of the fish that Maui had pulled out of the sea. Maui lived for a while on this great island with his wife Hina. Every day Hina went down to the swamp to fill her calabash.

One morning, as she bent over to dip into the water, there was a swirl in the pool, and a long writhing body shot up above the surface. It was Tuna-roa. The water dripped from him as he raised his head high in the air. Hina drew back and turned to run, but she was too late. Tuna's head darted forward and struck her between the shoulders so that she fell forward on her face. Tuna slipped out of the water and wrapped his slimy coils round her. Then he slid back to the water again.

Hina said nothing of this to her husband. The next day she watched carefully as she lowered the calabash. Again she saw something swimming up through the still, dark water. She dropped her calabash and ran, but her foot struck a stone and she fell. In an instant Tuna's damp body slid over her.

This time Hina told her husband. Maui was angry. He went into the forest and cast spells on the trees to make them do his will. Then he cut them down and made tools from them – spades that would dig deep and fast with none to set foot on them, spears that would sink easily into flesh, knives that would cut quickly. These he took to the swamp and set them working. The spades dug a broad ditch from the swamp to the sea. Maui stretched a net across the ditch and sat down to wait. Presently the rain fell. The little streams poured their water into the swamp. The water rose until it reached the ditch. It burst the narrow barrier of earth that the spades had left and roared down the trench. It carried great lumps of earth with it, tree trunks and plants, and in the middle of the torrent the struggling Tuna-roa.

He was tossed about, helpless in the turmoil of waters, until he felt himself caught in the meshes of the net. Then Maui raised his knife and slashed at Tuna's neck. The head fell off and was carried out to sea. Maui cut off his tail and, in his rage, chopped him into little pieces.

This was not the end of Tuna-roa. His head changed into a fish, his tail became the conger eel, and the little pieces changed into fresh-water eels. So Tuna-roa became the father of eels.

The years passed by and Maui grew older. He was as merry as ever, but there were silver threads in his hair, and his two sons were grown men. They were like their father. They were never serious, and Maui became jealous of them. One day he called them to him as the sun was setting. "My sons," he said, "I grow weary of the tale of your misdeeds. You bring shame upon me. The time has come for you to leave this world.

"But you will not be forgotten of men," he said, as he placed his hands on their shoulders. "I shall change you into stars. Who watches for the coming of night will see you, and you will be welcomed by those who look for the dawn. Farewell, my sons."

He touched them with his hand and their form changed, and they glowed with light. He took their jawbones to add to his store of fish-hooks. Maui lifted his sons in his hands and flung them far into space, until they took their place in the vast pattern of the sky. And there they are in the wide-flung cloak of Rangi, the Sky Father. One of them is the morning star and the other the evening star.

Among those who had watched the fate of the young men was Taki, an elder brother of Maui. Taki was old and weary. He saw the stars shining peacefully in the sky, and he longed for such rest himself. "Throw me into the sky as you have thrown my nephews," he begged. "Then I shall live for ever in the sight of men."

Maui looked at his brother thoughtfully. Taki's teeth were white and strong, even in his old age. Taki's jaw would make an excellent fish-hook. But Taki had become fat and heavy.

"I cannot throw you into the sky," Maui said. "But give me your jawbone and I will show you how to climb the spider's threads that stretch from earth to sky."

Taki agreed, and with Maui's help he climbed the dizzy heights. His eye grew brighter as he went to his place in the sky, and there he shines cheerfully for ever. He is Takiara, the guiding star.

Maui went fishing with Irawaru, the husband of his wife's sister. He had with him his famous fish-hook made from the jawbone of Muri. But in spite of its polished beauty, and its magic, Maui caught nothing, while Irawaru's hook brought fish after fish to join the silver heap on the bottom boards. Maui's temper began to fray.

Presently he felt a jerk on his line, and he pulled it in quickly.

In the place of Irawaru, there was a furry Maori dog,
the very first of dogs.

The two lines had crossed and Maui shouted, "Keep your hook free of my line. This is my fish." Irawaru paid out the cord to clear his hook, and both men pulled in their lines. When the fish lay gasping in the canoe it could be seen that it was on Irawaru's hook.

Maui concealed his anger. The canoe was paddled back to land, and when it reached the shore, Maui called to Irawaru to jump out and lift the outrigger. As he stooped and lifted it on his back, Maui threw down his paddle and leaped on to the heavy timber. Irawaru fell under the weight and lay helpless with the outrigger pressing him down on to the stones. Maui stamped on him until Irawaru's back became long. His skin grew furry, his arms and legs became short, a tail appeared, and his head changed in shape. In the place of Irawaru, there was a furry Maori dog, the very first of dogs.

Irawaru's wife met Maui as he came up from the beach. "Where is Irawaru?" she asked.

"I have left him by the canoe," Maui said with a laugh, though his eyes were not smiling. "Go down and help him, wife's sister. If you cannot find him, call him. Call 'Mo-i mo-i, mo-i', and he will answer."

The woman hurried to the beach but she could not see her husband. She called him, but there was no answer. Then she remembered Maui's words and she cried, "Mo-i, mo-i," and at once there was a rustle in the bushes and a strange animal ran out and frisked round her. When she saw it, Hinauri, the wife of Irawaru, turned back and walked in silence to the kainga, for she knew that Maui had taken vengeance on her husband, and her heart was sad.

Maui was growing old. His sons were among the stars that shone at night. The sun, as it moved slowly across the sky, reminded him of his boldness as a youth. He lived on the land he had pulled from the bed of the ocean. His evening meal was cooked with the fire he had stolen from Mahuika.

His people remembered these deeds. In spite of his evil temper, they remembered how much they owed to his impatience, and they looked to him to show them things more wonderful than these. And so, in his old age, Maui planned his greatest deed. He determined to conquer the dreadful goddess of death, Hine-nui-te-Po.

From far away he saw her. Her eyes shone, her teeth gleamed,

As Maui's friends watched, he failed in his last adventure
– to conquer the goddess of death.

the long masses of her hair flowed round her like surge-tossed seaweed, and when she spoke her voice rumbled like thunder.

Maui called to his friends the birds, and they flew to him. They came from sea and swamp and shore to do his bidding. He called for water, and Pukeko ran to fetch it. Maui was pleased, and he caught Pukeko and pulled his legs until they were long and thin, so that he could stride easily through the shallow waters of his native marshes. Only the birds were his friends as he drew near to the goddess.

Hine was asleep. Her mouth was wide open, and Maui threw off his cloak and made ready to crawl through her mouth.

"Listen," he whispered to the birds, "no one must laugh as I crawl through her mouth, even though the sight be strange. When I come out again, then you may laugh and sing, for I shall have killed the goddess, and men and birds need never die."

In the stillness Maui leaped head first into the body of Hine, through the entrance where men are born, and the frightened birds made no sound. Maui climbed further in until only his tattooed legs hung out. As he turned and twisted, his legs swung from side to side. Merry little Tiwaiwaka, the fantail, was watching and his shrill voice suddenly rang with the laughter he could not contain. Hine awoke. The lightning flashed from her red eyes and her teeth came together with a mighty crash.

It was only the laugh of Tiwaiwaka, the little fantail who laughs no more; only that, and an incantation that his father forgot, that prevented Maui from overcoming death.

For a day and a night the birds were sad and silent when they remembered their friend, Maui. And then they forgot, for life is too short to be spent in sorrow, and death at the end is like sleep that comes to the weary.

5

Tawhaki the Bold

On a flat reef of rocks which thrust itself through the swell of the waves and the surging bull-kelp, Tawhaki and his four brothers-in-law were fishing. As they pulled in the flax lines with the bone hooks, the heaps of fish behind them grew into piles of shining silver. But when the sun began to sink, Tawhaki's pile was as great as those of the four brothers put together.

Tawhaki laughed as he gathered them into his basket, and began to taunt his brothers. They had no reply to make, but in their minds they were yet more firmly resolved to carry out the plan that had been decided upon when they invited him to come with them. The real trouble was jealousy. Tawhaki was the most skilled of all their tribe in the arts of peace and war, in running and swimming, in fighting and love-making. As he shouldered his basket, he began to sing, for he could not read his brothers' minds.

Two of them reached the village as the sun dipped below the sea. Their sister met them as they dropped their loaded baskets. "Where is my husband?" she asked.

"We left him with our brothers," they said quickly, like people who have been expecting a question and have an answer in their minds all the time. Their sister looked at them closely and frowned. She felt there was something strange in the way they spoke. They had hardly been civil to her husband for weeks on end, but that morning they had come early to her whare and with smooth words had persuaded Tawhaki to go fishing with them. She looked at their baskets, stuffed to overflowing with fish. Everyone knew that her brothers were poor fishermen.

She hurried down to the beach, where she met her other brothers.

"Where is my husband?"

Her voice was sharp, and the laughter of her brothers sounded

The gods gave strength to
the wife of Tawhaki.

false even in their own ears as they said: "Why do you ask us? He went home with our brothers. We are not his guardians."

She did not reply, but broke into a run, following the mark of footsteps in the sand. It was getting dark, but the footprints still showed faintly, just above the white line of the waves. Fear was in her heart as she ran. The shadow of the rocky headland lay dark upon the sand, and in it was a darker shape. She fell on her knees beside it. It was Tawhaki. She put her face close to his and felt the gentle stirring of his breath, so faint it was almost lost in the hissing of the little waves as they lapped his outstretched arm. She raised his head and he stirred and opened his eyes. A smile curved his lips.

"Your brothers –" he said faintly. "They lack skill in battle as well as in sport. They thought they had killed me."

His head fell back again. The gods gave strength to the wife of Tawhaki. She lifted her husband in her arms and slid the dead weight of his body round on to her back. He weighed heavy on her but she bent her back until his feet were lifted clear of the sand. In this fashion, planting one foot heavily after another, she returned along the faint tracks her flying feet had made in the sand.

Tawhaki did not open his eyes until the morning. "Is there a tall tree near the whare?" he asked abruptly. "Bring it here and put it on the fire." His wife dragged a great log out of the bush.

"Do not cut it up," Tawhaki said. "Put it on the fire as it is."

While the flames licked the bark, he stretched out his hands to the blaze. "As the fire eats the wood, so shall my children eat the children of your brothers," he said, his eyes reflecting the fierce glare of the fire. "When our son is born he shall be named Wahieroa to remind him of the will of his father. Long-log-of-wood-for-the-fire shall be his name."

Months went by and a son was born to Tawhaki. His name was Wahieroa.

Tawhaki called his own relatives and warriors together. "Faithless are the people of this village," he said. "We shall take our families with us and build a pa of our own. Let us go to the summit where the last gleams of sunlight linger. Let us go now, while the faithless ones skulk in their whares. None shall dare to hinder us in our going, and we shall have no pity on them."

On the top of the mountain they built their pa. Its treble line of palisades could be seen against the morning sky with the sentries standing on their towers. At night the cries of the watchers floated across the bush-clad valleys, even as far as the village by the sea where the brothers took their careless ease. They were happier now that Tawhaki had gone, and even the sharp silhouette of the palisades that hung in the sky failed to disturb their quietness of mind.

But Tawhaki had not forgotten. The sight of the little Wahieroa, lying in his mother's arms, reminded him of his promise. "Revenge must not be left to my son," he reflected. "The injury is mine and vengeance is mine."

He climbed up to the highest part of the mountain where the clouds seemed to float at arm's length. He lifted his arms and called on the gods, his ancestors, to release the floods of heaven. The clouds dropped closer to the earth, heavy and black. The wind died down and a stillness lay over the land. Then the waters of heaven emptied themselves. The little streams became roaring torrents, but the noise of the hurrying water was drowned by the drumming of the rain. Out at sea the calm water had been turned into a mass of white spume, and as the hungry rivers hurled themselves into the sea, the little waves, faster than any tide, crept up the sand to the village where the murderers were crouching in the shelter of their whares. They watched the water creeping over the high ridge of grass-bound sand. It swirled across the marae and gurgled round their feet. It heaped itself in a long slow curve, and before they could leave their doorways, it rose silently to the tekoteko on the roof-tree and shut out the sound of their cries.

The last raindrops fell from the clouds and the sun shone again on a crazy world of intermingled forest and tossing sea. Looking through the steam that rose from every sodden tree and hill, Tawhaki could see the water slowly ebbing away from the village at the foot of the mountain. The tekotekos thrust their grinning heads above the waves, but the thatch of the whares had been carried away by the silent water, and with it the bodies of the brothers of his wife. Only the gaunt framework of the whares showed where the faithless ones had lived.

The water rose silently to the tekoteko
on the roof-free.

Some time after the great flood, Tawhaki thought of his parents who had been stolen many years before by the Ponaturi, the strange people who sleep on land at night, but who fear the sun and go down below the sea before daylight comes. He felt that he must leave home and seek them.

Taking his younger brother, Karihi, with him, he left the hilltop home and began his search. No one knew where the Ponaturi lived. Tawhaki said to his brother: "Their sleeping-place must lie somewhere near the shore, for they will not dare to go far from the sea. We must seek for them along the coast."

They travelled a long way and slept many times. One day they crossed a ridge which gave them a view of the curving beach ahead. A huge whare stood by itself not far from the shore. There were no buildings to be seen except this solitary whare, the ridge-pole of which towered far above the forest trees at its side.

"The home of the Ponaturi!" Tawhaki exclaimed. "I know it, for there are thousands of the sea-creatures, and until now no house we have seen would be big enough to hold them all."

The two brothers walked boldly along the grass that bordered the sand, for it was mid-day and the Ponaturi were hidden in the dark valleys below the ocean. Tawhaki sang an ancient chant as they drew near. Then they stopped to listen. Somewhere near the top of the whare they heard the faint rattling of bones. Tawhaki's hair bristled like a dog's. "They are the bones of our father," he said to Karihi. "They are rattling with gladness because we have come. Our father knows that vengeance is at hand."

"This is indeed the house of Manawa-tane," Karihi replied. "And there is our mother standing at the door."

The old woman wept as she recognised her sons. She embraced them, and when her weeping had come to an end she spoke. "You must return to your home at once," she said. "Your father was killed by the sea-people; my children must not be lost."

"We shall not return till we have avenged our father," Tawhaki said firmly. "We have heard the bones proclaim his joy; we are not to be turned aside from our resolve."

"You cannot stand against them, my sons," his mother said sadly. "Go now while there is time."

Karihi spoke. "We are determined. You shall hide us in the whare."

"That will not serve you well, my sons. They will see you even in the dark."

"We shall make ourselves invisible," Karihi said.

"They will smell the man-scent."

"That we shall see," Tawhaki spoke abruptly. "This is what you shall do, my mother."

His mother bowed her head. She helped her sons to block up the holes and chinks in the walls of the whare and watched them climb into the thick thatch that covered the roof.

They were hidden when night fell and the first of the Ponaturi put his head through the door.

"Tatau!" he called. "I can smell the man-scent."

"That is nonsense," she replied. "There is no one but old Tatau here."

The scout was not satisfied, but while he sniffed round the walls the Ponaturi came crowding up the beach, shaking the water from them and pressing into the whare. They lay down on the floor, and the scout lay down with them, for the man-scent had been lost in the crowd.

The hours of the night passed slowly while Tatau sat in the darkness outside the door. Occasionally an old man would stir and call out: "Ho, Tatau, Tatau, there; is the dawn coming?"

She would answer: "No, no, it is deep night; it is lasting night; it is still night; sleep soundly; sleep on."

Presently the glowing fingers of the dawn began to spread over the eastern sky and the stars had paled before them. Tawhaki and Karihi stood beside their mother and listened. A voice called: "Ho, Tatau, surely the dawn is coming?"

The old lady replied: "No, no, it is night; it is lasting night; it is still night; sleep soundly; sleep on."

Rangi's mantle of daylight spread from east to west and the sun shone brightly on Manawa-tane. Several voices cried impatiently: "Tatau! Tatau! The dawn must be near. Is it not light yet?"

At a sign from her sons, Tatau shouted: "Yes, it is light!"

She pulled the door away while Tawhaki and Karihi leaped to the window and burst through the reed walls so that the sunlight

The brothers took their father's bones and
set fire to the house of the Ponaturi.

flooded the house. The Ponaturi had risen to their feet, but the sunbeams smote them before they could stir from their places, and they melted away like mist. Not a single one of them remained. Only the kanae, the salmon, escaped, leaping and bounding through the broken walls and across the sand to the water, even as he does to this day when he climbs the waterfalls of the rivers.

The brothers took their father's bones reverently from the roof-tree and wrapped them up. They set fire to the tall house of the Ponaturi and led their mother away. As they crossed the ridge they looked back and saw the last charred timbers settling down in the greying ashes. A thin column of smoke rising in the air was the only thing left to make the grave of the myriad Ponaturi, the fish-men of Manawa-tane.

The years passed by and Tawhaki was lonely. His mother and his wife had gone to the Reinga, and his son had taken a wife. But Tawhaki's fame had spread afar, even up to the heavenly places. Looking down from her home in the sky, a daughter of the gods who had heard of his mighty deeds saw the strength of his limbs, the muscles that rippled under his skin, the deep tattooing, the fire that glowed in his eyes, the clear-cut features, the way he walked, the fearless manner of his talking.

She came down from the seventh heaven and lived with Tawhaki. In time a daughter was born to them, descendant of the immortal woman and the mortal father. They lived happily together until one day, in a thoughtless moment, Tawhaki made a careless remark about his daughter that wounded his celestial wife. She was not like a woman of earth. She caught her child up in her arms and rose up towards the sky. Tawhaki realised the consequences of his words. Hapai, his wife, had risen beyond his reach. For a moment she rested by the tekoteko at the roof gable and looked sorrowfully at her husband. "I shall never come back," she said.

"Tell me then what I may have as a remembrance of you," Tawhaki cried.

Hapai remained silent for a little space. "You will follow, Tawhaki, I know it. My message to you is this: When you climb the heights of heaven, beware of the creeper that sways in the wind.

Choose the one whose roots have struck deeply into the earth. Farewell."

The moon had swelled, night by night, and diminished night by night until it was but a line of silver in the sky.

"Come Karihi," Tawhaki said to his brother. "Let us go out again together."

"Where shall we go?" asked Karihi.

"A long way, brother. I am going to search for my wife and daughter."

The brothers travelled together far over the land until they saw the tendrils that stretched like the threads of a giant spider's web between earth and heaven. They hurried towards them, and there, holding the tendrils in her hand, sat their old, blind grandmother, Matakerepo. Ten taro roots were spread in front of her. Tawhaki and Karihi cam up quietly and watched the old lady. With her free hand she felt the roots and counted them slowly: "One, two, three, four, five, six, seven, eight, nine –" With a twinkle in his eye Tawhaki had quietly removed the tenth root. A puzzled frown wrinkled the old woman's brow. Thinking she had counted them wrongly, she began again. "One, two, three, four, five, six, seven, eight –" This time Karihi had taken a root.

Matakerepo grumbled to herself and once more she felt the roots. "One, two, three, four, five, six, seven –" For a moment she sat silent in thought. Someone was stealing her roots. With a lightning move she snatched up a weapon and lashed round her in a wide circle with a blow that would have laid open a man's skull. Tawhaki and Karihi were watching her like hawks and as the weapon sang through the air they lay flat on their faces so that it passed harmlessly over them.

Their grandmother put the weapon away and sat wrapped in thought. Tawhaki crept forward and struck her playfully on the face. The old woman was frightened. Releasing the tendril she had been holding, she put her hands to her face and cried pitifully: "Who is it? Who is there?"

Tawhaki struck her again across her eyes and immediately her sight was restored. Blinking in the unaccustomed light, she peered into the faces of the men in front of her. Then she gave a loud cry of welcome.

Matakerepo lashed round in a wide circle
as Tawhai and Karihi lay flat on their faces.

"It is you, Tawhaki, my grandson, and Karihi."

She embraced them both. When greetings were over, she asked them where they were going.

"I am searching for my daughter and wife," Tawhaki said.

"Where are they?"

"They are above, somewhere in the Sky-land."

The old lady blinked. "What made them go to the sky, Tawhaki?"

"Hapai was a goddess, my grandmother. She came down to earth and lived with me for a while, but now she has returned. The days are empty without wife or daughter, so I have come to seek them."

"There lies your ladder to the skies," his grandmother replied, grasping the creepers again. "That is the road you must travel. Beware the tendrils that sway in the breeze; and when you are between heaven and earth, my grandson, do not look down lest you become giddy. Look ever up."

Karihi had been looking up at the creepers. Without waiting to hear his grandmother's words, he sprang up and clutched one of them; but it was one which was drifting loosely above the earth. The moment his fingers closed on the rope-like stem a gust of wind caught it and swept him out of sight. His breath choked him as the forests and seas raced below in a flashing pattern of green and blue. A moment later another fierce gust swung up towards the sky. He dropped with a sickening jolt that almost tore his hands away. Again he was swept out towards the horizon. Again he was swept back. Far off he could see Tawhaki and Matakerepo. They grew suddenly large and Tawhaki shouted: "Let go now." As the creeper swept past Karihi dropped off and fell at the feet of his brother.

Tawhaki felt alarmed for his brother's safety. It was not a light thing to undertake, this storming of the citadel of the gods. In his heart he knew Karihi was not fitted to face the dangers of the long journey to the heavens.

"Go home to our people, Karihi," he said kindly. "Our families need protection. Go back to the pa while there is time, for I may not return, and it is better than one chief should be lost rather than two."

Karihi felt that his brother was right. He longed to dare that stupendous climb, but Tawhaki knew best, and sadly he returned to the pa upon the hill-top.

Tawhaki chose the firmly-rooted creeper carefully and grasped the stem in his strong hands. He climbed steadily, clinging firmly with his toes as well as his fingers. He kept his eyes fixed on the creeper where it thinned to a thread in the bright sky and was lost to sight. His grandmother's voice came up to him, fainter and ever fainter as he climbed, but it gave him new strength. "Hold fast, Tawhaki, hold fast. Let your hands hold fast." Presently the voice faded away and there was no sound but the singing of the tendril in the air, and the never-ceasing whisper of the winds, the restless children of Tawhiri-matea. He longed to see the comforting earth and perhaps that distant speck that would be Matakerepo, but he continued to look upwards. It was cold in empty space, but he chanted the incantation that gave strength to his hands and warmth to his body.

Before he could realise it, Tawhaki found himself in the Sky-land, lying among the ferns and breathing heavily. Presently he stood up and looked round. The trees grew close together and there was no one in sight. but he could hear the thud of an axe and the sound of voices. He changed himself into the form of an old man, white hair, thin and stooped, and pushed through the undergrowth.

He came to the edge of a clearing and stood watching the scene. An unfinished canoe lay on the ground and a score of god-men were busy on it, cutting and smoothing the long hull. They were the brothers of Hapai, his celestial wife, and Tawhaki knew that he was coming to the end of his search.

They stopped their work to look at him as he approached. One of them shouted: "Look at the old man there. Come, it is nearly night. Let us finish now. The old man can carry our tools."

They threw down their axes and one of them addressed Tawhaki: "Come, slave, pick up the axes and follow us as quickly as you can."

Tawhaki picked up the tools and followed the chattering god-men. He limped amidst the shadows and soon they were out of sight. Then he turned and hurried back to the canoe. Throwing off his cloak, he took an adze and putting the sharp edge to the rough wood, he ran it swiftly along the sides. The wood curled crisply from the greenstone blade and instead of the uneven timber a smooth surface slid from under the planing edge. Several times

An unfinished canoe lay on the ground
and a score of god-men were busy on it.

Tawhaki laid the adze blade to the huge log and in a few minutes the shape of a finished hull grew under his cunning fingers.

As he approached the village where the brothers of Hapai lived, old and decrepit and bent under his load of axes, he met two women who had been gathering wood for the fire. "Here is the new slave they have been telling us about," one of them laughed. "Why should we carry wood when there is a slave to do it for us. Come, old man, come over here."

Tawhaki went to them and stooped while they laid a bundle of sticks on his back. And so he came to the home of his wife, Tawhaki the warrior-chief who was without peer in the Earth-land, stooped as an old man, dishonoured as a slave. They laughed at him as he crossed the marae. He saw his wife and daughter but he made no sign. Still bending under his load, he walked steadily towards them.

"Put the wood down there, low-born," someone shouted, but Tawhaki took no notice. He walked straight on towards Hapai as she sat warming herself by the fire, and threw the wood close beside her. Then he lowered himself to the ground, slowly and carefully as an old man will, and held out his hands to the blaze.

"Fool!" a young man shouted. "You have made yourself tapu by sitting so close to the high-born Hapai."

Tawhaki did not answer but stared at his wife and child through the leaping flames; but they took no notice of the old man who lay back in the darkness of their home.

The next morning Tawhaki was awakened by a cry: "Get up, slave, and take the tools to the canoe."

Like an old man he straightened his back slowly and stood up. He picked up the adzes and followed the god-men through the bush to the canoe. As they came into the clearing he heard their shout of surprise and smiled to himself. They took no notice of him when he lowered the tools to the ground and listened to their exclamations as they walked round the half-finished canoe, looking at the work that had been done since they left the previous night.

When the dusk began to creep down on the clearing, the god-men left their work with little to show for the day's toil, and Tawhaki followed with the adzes. When they were out of sight, he returned once more with swift steps and adzed and planed until the canoe was nearly finished.

The following morning there was even more talk and bewilderment. At nightfall Tawhaki returned to the clearing and added the last strokes to the delicate whorls on the prow and the stern-post. He had shed his disguise, and as he reached up to the lofty column of wooden tracery at the stern, he looked like a god. Keen eyes were staring at him out of the undergrowth, for this time his brothers-in-law had remained hidden behind the bushes to watch for the coming of the skilled worker who had completed their task. Without a word they hurried to their village and sought out their sister, Hapai.

"Tell us," they said, "what does your husband look like? Is he a man in the fullness of his strength?"

"Ae."

"Tall and straight as a kauri?"

"Ae."

"Is his hair black and his eyes like stars?"

"Ae."

"Then it is Tawhaki who has finished our canoe. Watch you for him when he comes."

Presently the old man walked on to the marae and lowered the adzes from his back. He walked towards Hapai. She looked at him carefully. This man's back was bent. He face seemed wrinkled and the flesh hung in loose folds on his body.

"Who are you?" asked Hapai.

The old man walked on without a word.

"Tell me, are you Tawhaki?"

He continued on until he reached Hapai's daughter. He lifted her up and held her tightly in his arms. As he straightened himself his limbs filled out and the muscles rippled again on his broad back. When he turned to Hapai his face had become young and handsome, and the fires of joy were shining in his eyes.

"It is Tawhaki!" the god-men cried, but Hapai lowered her head and cried, for her heart was melting with gladness.

Tawhaki took his place in the whare with his wife that night. When the sun rose they broke down the wall of their home and carried the little girl through the place where no feet had walked before, and she was baptised. Her father was there, bold Tawhaki among the god-men. Thunder and lightning broke from the ground beneath his feet when he walked.

When the lightning flashes and the thunder roars through the heavens, men listen and look up at the lofty sky and say to each other: "It is Tawhaki who walks in the heavens."

6

Rupe the Kind Brother

Hina-Uri, whose husband the madcap Maui had turned into a dog, had thrown herself into the sea in her grief. The tides washed her to and fro, and at length cast her up on to a sandy beach. She was found by two brothers. Under the barnacles and tangled seaweed that had grown over her, they could see that she was young and beautiful.

They lifted her tenderly and carried her to their home. She was set down by the fire, and the growths that had covered her were scraped off. Presently, as the warmth of the fire revived her, she sat up and spread her hands to the blaze. In the gentle heat her wrinkled skin tightened and the colour came into her face and hands. When they saw that she had recovered, the young men went to their chief, Tinirau, and told him of the young woman who had come from the sea. Tinirau hastened to their whare, and as soon as he saw Hina-uri, he said, "She shall be my wife," and in spite of her protests he took her back to live with him.

Hina-uri was unhappy in Tinirau's whare. She still loved her husband, and her sorrow increased within her daily, for Tinirau had two other wives who hated her. They insulted her and called her names and even went so far as to strike her, and to make plans to kill her. Hina-uri, who was of the same blood as Maui, refused to submit to these indignities, and one day she rose and chanted a powerful incantation to the gods. The birds and insects fell silent as her chant rose in the cold morning air. Even the leaves of the trees ceased their endless whispering, and Tinirau's wives felt their blood running cold in their veins. As the chant ended they swayed and fell, and lay cold and lifeless on the ground with their feet pointing up.

Tinirau took no notice of them. He led Hina-uri back to his

At the chanting of Hina-uri, the wives of Tinirau
fell lifeless to the ground.

whare and gazed on her beauty, but Hina-uri stared back at him with unseeing eyes.

Far away, Maui-mua, the brother of Hina-uri, was sad. He had sought her far and wide, but no one could tell him where she had gone. While he was still grieving for her, a sudden thought came into his mind. "The great god Rehua who lives in the tenth heaven is my ancestor," he reflected. "I will seek him, for surely he can tell me where I may find Hina-uri."

The tenth heaven was far away, and Maui the first-born could reach it only by flying as a bird. With magic spells and incantations he changed himself into a pigeon, into the gentle Rupe, and breasted the thin air. After a time he came to the first heaven and asked the people there whether he might fly higher still. They shouted in anger because a bird had dared to think of piercing the heavens which Tane had sewed together; but Rupe was rested after his long flight, and he flew upwards again, brushing past the hands that were stretched out to seize him.

At last he reached the highest heaven where Rehua, the god of kindness, lived. As Rupe looked at his face he knew that he would help him. He bowed before him and told him of his long search for his sister. Rehua embraced him and ordered his servants to cook food for the weary wanderer. They brought empty calabashes and set them before him. Then as Rupe looked on in amazement, Rehua unbound his long hair and shook it over the calabashes. As he did so many birds flew out and were caught by the servants and cooked.

But Rupe was reluctant to eat the birds that had come from the sacred hair of Rehua, and he refused to eat the delicious food, though it is true that some people say he did eat them, and that for this reason his voice became hoarse, and remains so to this day.

Rupe asked the god of kindness if he had ever heard the noise of voices in the world below, and Rehua replied, "In the Sacred Isle (Motu-tapu) have I heard the constant sound of voices, and there you may find your sister."

Rupe did not delay. He flew down the ten heavens to Motu-tapu, and there he perched on a window-sill and watched the people to see if his sister was among them. Hina-uri was indeed on the Sacred Isle. That very day her little baby had been born and she was nursing him in the cool shelter of a nearby house. Presently she heard people running and shouting, "Hina! Hina! Come and see the pigeon who has bewitched our warriors."

She looked through the doorway and saw a pigeon on the window-sill of a whare. The people were throwing stones at it and trying to spear it. A young man had nearly slipped a flax noose over its head, but the pigeon hopped warily from side to side, and not a stone or spear could touch him, while the flax noose slipped from him. Hina-uri picked up her baby and walked over to see the strange sight.

Rupe saw her coming and knew his sister at once. As he danced from side to side, he sang clearly:

> It is Hina,
> It is Hina,
> Who was lost
> At Motu-tapu.
> Yes, truly
> She is here.

Hina-uri then knew that the pigeon was her brother, Maui-mua. She hurried towards him, singing as she went:

> It is Rupe,
> It is Rupe,
> The elder brother.
> Yes, truly,
> He is here.

Rupe saw that she was unhappy on the Sacred Isle, and he flew with her up to the tenth heaven, to Rehua's home. There they lived happily for long years, and Rupe kept Rehua's home free of dust and dirt. That is the story of Rupe the pigeon. We may not often see his beautiful plumage, but we may remember him when we see the sunset, for Rupe, as keeper of Rehua's house, set up a post in the tenth heaven, over which Kai-tangata, the man-eater, fell. It is his blood which spreads over the sky and often stains it a vivid red at the time of the setting of the sun.

7

Rata the Wanderer

This is the story of Rata, the grandson of Tawhaki and his earthly wife. When Rata became a man he set out on a long journey to the home of Matuku who, many years before, had killed his father. All his life Rata had trained himself in the arts of war ready for the day when he should avenge the death of his father.

He took with him a band of young warriors. When they reached the home of Matuku, Rata repeated spells to protect them from witchcraft. Matuku was away from home. Only an old woman was there, who helped them with their plans.

"Light a fire," she said, "and Matuku will hurry home to see why it has been lit. Now do you hang a noose over the door and as soon as he comes in it will drop over his shoulders and secure him by the waist. It is useless to catch him by the neck, for it is strong. There is not so much strength in his waist."

Rata and his warriors soon had a fire blazing, and before long the ground began to shake. Matuku was hurrying home. The fighting men were hidden on either side of the doorway waiting for him to enter. When he was a few steps away he halted abruptly and sniffed with his long nose.

"Ah!" he cried. "I smell men, living men!"

"No," the old woman called out, "it is nothing. Hurry in."

But Matuku was suspicious.

"It is fresh meat I smell. There is danger in the air."

"No, no," the woman cried. "It is nothing. It is only the flesh you are carrying on your back that you can smell."

So Matuku came in. The noose dropped lightly over his shoulders, and as he started back the warriors hauled on the rope. It tightened with a jerk and Matuku was swung off his feet.

"Ha-a!" shouted Rata as he rushed forward. "You have murdered my father. Now you will also be murdered."

But Matuku only laughed.

"You cannot kill me," he shouted. Rata slashed at him with his mere and cut off one arm, then the other. Matuku laughed again. His voice boomed louder than ever in the narrow confines of the house. Rata raised his mere for the third time, and with one clean blow he severed Matuku's head.

While the triumphant warriors loosed the flax ropes, Matuku's voice suddenly boomed out again. His legs grew thin, the long hair that covered his body changed to feathers, he became smaller and slipped out of the ropes. He had changed into a bittern. Running past the astonished men, he vanished into the night. They could not see him, but far away in the swamp they heard his booming voice.

He still booms in the lonely swamps, for Matuku is the name of the bittern of the swamps.

The old woman appeared again as the bittern ran to the swamp, a toothless smile on her face. "It is good," she said simply. "Now I can take my rest."

Rata went up to her. "Tell me," he said, "where are the bones of Wahieroa, my father?"

"They are not here."

"Where are they?"

The old woman peered at him and replied, "No one can tell."

"Who took them away?"

"A strange people. They live far away," she said vaguely.

Rata returned to his home with the fighting men and for days he sat in the whare, lost in thought. When he came out there was new life in his step. He had thought of a plan. If he could build a canoe and endow it with strength and wisdom, it would carry him to the place where his father's bones had been taken.

He searched for a tall, straight tree, and when he found one that pleased him, he laid his axe to it. The edge of the greenstone bit into the hard wood and in a little time the tree crashed through the undergrowth and thundered to the ground. Rata cut off its green head.

Then it was night, and he returned to the kainga. While he slept, strange things happened in the forest. The children of Tane were angry that this tree, the pride of the forest, should have been

The birds and insects raised the tree and fitted
the branches and chips of wood into place.

cut down. The children of Tane are like the grains of sand on the shore in number – more than can be counted by men. Only Tane can tell how many there are. The bush was alive with them, riro and kuku, korimako and tui, hihi and kaka, kokako and huia, popokotea and mohua and many others, and with them all the family of insects, those that run about on the bark of trees and under the leaves, those on the ground and those with wings. They gathered themselves together and pulled at the forest giant. It stirred uneasily on its grassy bed and the air was filled with the whirring of wings; slowly it rose upright and stood in its own place. The smallest insects carried the chips and grains of wood and fitted them in place.

> *Fly together, chips and shavings,*
> *Stick ye fast together,*
> *Hold ye fast together;*
> *Stand upright again, o tree!*

It was the song of myriads of insects and birds.

When Rata returned in the morning to begin the work of shaping the canoe, he rubbed his eyes. For a moment he thought he had mistaken his direction, but this he could not believe for he was wise in the ways of the forest. When he looked around him he could see the broken branches and leaves of the undergrowth, and even the unmistakable groove where the trunk of the tree had pressed into the ground; but there it stood where it had been growing for many times the life-span of a man.

Rata chanted an incantation to protect himself against the spirits before taking up his axe and cutting down the tree again. He worked swiftly and soon the tree lay prone with its head severed, and his adze sped along the straight trunk, taking off the long curling shavings, like that of his grandfather in the Sky-land so many years before. By nightfall the graceful lines of the canoe had been shaped out of the timber and only the hollowing of the hull remained to be done.

But when he returned the next morning, not a sign of his work remained. Throughout the moonlit night the children of Tane had laboured at the raising of the tree until it stood proudly lifting its waving branches above the lesser trees of the forest.

For the third time Rata hewed at the bole of the tree and for the third time it crashed to the ground. Without troubling to work any further at it, Rata picked up his axe and went towards the village. When he was out of sight of the tree he turned from the track and slipped noiselessly through the clustering ferns until he could see the place where the tree was resting.

The low-pitched, reverberating song came to his ears.

> Fly together, chips and shavings,
> Stick ye fast together,
> Hold ye fast together;
> Stand upright again, o tree!

It was like the sound of the bush in summertime, a throbbing melody that set the air itself quivering. He could see the flash of wings. Never had there been so many forest birds together at one time. The weka and the kiwi ran round the fallen tree; the fantail fluttered anxiously over it, ruru and kaka and kakapo and thousands of others were pulling and tugging at it. He looked closer and saw insects running to and fro, falling over each other in their eagerness to help. The singing deepened in tone, throbbing like the huge greenstone gong in the pa.

Rata felt the force of that many-tongued incantation. His own feet seemed almost to leave the ground. Before his startled gaze the tree rose upwards, hidden under a canopy of birds. It stood up straight with the sharpened point of the trunk, where his axe had bitten into it, resting lightly on the point of the stump. Insects swarmed upwards from the ground, fitting the tiniest splinters accurately into place.

"Ha!" cried Rata, springing up and rushing towards the tree, "it is you who have undone my work."

The birds crowded round him. "It is you, Rata, you who have dared to fell the forest god. We are the protectors of the garden of Tane."

Then Rata felt ashamed of working against these little loved ones of Tane.

"What shall I do?" he asked. "My heart yearned for a canoe of grace and power that I might honour my ancestors and bring back the bones of my father to their resting place."

The song of the forest guardians swelled again. "Return to your place, Rata. We will make your canoe."

Rata turned away and left the building of the mighty canoe to the tiny forest people. In a day it was made – Riwaru, the Great Joy.

It was dragged through the forest on sapling skids and launched on the waves. Proud and stately it rode, and within its strong bulwarks there was room for a hundred and forty men. They took their places, the fighting men of Rata, and plied their paddles until Riwaru skimmed the waves like a gull as it flies above the water, lifting to the incoming waves.

The creaming wake lay behind them, straight and broad, and soon they were in sight of the shore where the Ponaturi lived, the enemy who had taken the bones of Wahieroa.

At nightfall Rata swam to the beach alone, leaving the canoe floating off-shore. There were lights on the beach close to the forest, where the fires of the Ponaturi burned. Rata hid behind the flax bushes and watched. He felt the makutu in his bones. There was strong magic round the fires. The hairs on his neck bristled, for the tohungas of the Ponaturi were knocking the bones of his father together to assist them in their arts.

They chanted their powerful incantations and the strong magic flowered in the firelight. Rata lay motionless, learning by heart the words of the karakia. When it had entered into him so that it could not be forgotten, he leapt to his feet and sprang among them with his mere in his hand. The tohungas were unprepared. Their magic had not revealed the enemy lying so close at hand. The bones of Wahieroa had not betrayed his son. In a moment or two, while the flames ate through a stick and a charred fragment fell into the ash, the tohungas lay still.

Rata gathered the bones together by the light of the dying fires and returned swiftly to his canoe. At sunrise Riwaru ran lightly up the beach in front of Rata's village.

When the Ponaturi came to the tuahu they found the tohungas lying stiff and cold in the morning sunlight, and the bones of Wahieroa gone.

"Rata!" they cried, "Rata, son of Wahieroa, has done this thing." They gathered together at once and manning their canoes a thousand strong they followed the path of Riwaru until they reached the village.

A mighty battle was fought there, and sixty of Rata's men fell before the surge of the Ponaturi. A dozen of the Ponaturi surrounded every man and the battle turned against the defenders.

Rata heard a stirring in the pa. The bones of Wahieroa had a message for him. Suddenly he remembered the karakia he had heard from the tohungas, the night they met death. He chanted it boldly and his dead warriors rose to their feet, the life blood running through their veins again. The Ponaturi faltered as they met the weapons of their slain enemy. They looked around them and then turned and ran for the canoes, but too late. Of the thousand Ponaturi not one returned to tell the tale.

That is the story of Rata. Because of his courage, the little people of the forest came to his aid. Countless times the bright sun has lifted himself above the rim of the sea since the day they helped Rata in his quest, but they have not changed. To those who love the garden of Tane, the children of Tane are kind; but where the lovely children of the forest god are driven away, there the winds of Tawhiri-matea sweep through the land and the tears of the Sky-father fall, washing away the fertile soil, leaving the bare bones of Mother Earth that are unable to nourish any living thing.

Children of Aotearoa, remember!

8

Uenuku and the Mist Girl

As he walked along the narrow path between the trees, Uenuku stared at the column of mist hovering over the lake. He had often seen mist lying low on the water but never a column of it standing up like the trunk of a tall tree. He quickened his step, overcome with curiosity. At the edge of the forest, close to the beach, he stopped. Two young women were bathing in the still water. He could see that they were beautiful even through the veils of mist which were wrapped round them like a cloud. Further out the air was clear, but nearer to the shore everything had turned to silver in the clinging cloud. These two women were Hine-pukohu-rangi, the Girl of the Mist, and her sister Hine-wai, the Misty Rain Girl. They had come down from the sky to bathe in the clear water of the lake.

As he looked at them Uenuku felt a strange sensation come over him. He seemed drawn to them by a powerful force. They looked at him with clear eyes, unafraid and wondering. Uenuku knelt down at the water's edge and said to the Mist Girl, "I am Uenuku. Tell me your name."

"I am Hine-pukohu-rangi, daughter of the sky. I am the Girl of the Mist,"

Uenuku stretched out his arms. "Come and live with me in this world of light," he said. "I have never seen a woman so beautiful as you. I am strong and will take care of you."

"I cannot leave my home," the Mist Girl replied. "Even now my sister is waiting for me to return."

"Ah, you will love this world," Uenuku pleaded. "It is not cold and empty like the space above. There is fire and warmth here, with the summer sun shining through the leaves of the trees and in winter the glowing fire on the hearth. There are birds and their

Uenuku stretched out his arms
to the Girl of the Mist.

songs, men and women and their laughter. Come with me, Girl of the Mist."

She took a step towards him and then drew back. "You would not be happy with me," she said.

"I would always love you," Uenuku said simply.

"But you do not understand. I come from the Outer Space, and though I might spend the night with you, I should have to return to my home in the heavens as soon as the sky grew light."

Uenuku was stubborn. "I still want you," he said. "Even though I shall be lonely during the day, please come and live with me."

The Mist Girl smiled. "I will come with you," she said.

No one saw Uenuku and his bride as they slipped into the whare when the firelight glowed in the creeping darkness. No one heard his words of love as he took her into his arms. In the morning, before the sun had risen over the hills, the Mist Girl met her sister. They seemed to mingle like two clouds and drifted upwards before the sun's rays could pierce them.

Every morning the Mist Girl left her husband and every evening she joined him when the shadows stole across the marae. As the summer days grew longer the women of the pa began to poke fun at Uenuku.

"You say you have a bride in your whare," they laughed. "Where is your bride, Uenuku, this bride we have never seen? Perhaps she is only a log of wood or a bundle of korari. Show her to us and we will believe you when you say she is beautiful."

There was only a little time between the sinking of the sun and his rising again. During the long hours of daylight Uenuku missed the laughter of the Mist Girl and longed to hear her voice lifted up in song, and to see her take her place among the poi-dancers.

In the end he could bear the absence of his wife no longer. One day he tied mats across the windows and pushed moss into the crevices between the planks. When the door was shut the whare was as dark as a moonless night when the clouds have covered the sky.

That night the Mist Girl entered the whare unsuspectingly. The hours of darkness passed until the first light flushed the eastern sky and the Rain Girl called to her sister.

"Come, Hine, we must rise up from the earth."

"I am coming," the Mist Girl answered and felt round in the darkness for her cloak.

"What are you doing?" Uenuku asked.

"It is time for me to go."

"Nonsense," he replied, pretending to be half asleep. "Why are you disturbing me? Look around you, there is no light anywhere."

"But morning must be near. My sister has called me."

"Hine-wai is mistaken. Perhaps she has seen the moonlight or the starlight. There is no light anywhere. Go to sleep again."

Hine-pukohu-rangi lay down. "She must be mistaken," she said, "but it is strange. I do not understand it. She has never made such a mistake before."

The Misty Rain Girl kept on calling and her voice was mingled with the sound of the waking birds, but Uenuku maintained that she was mistaken. Presently she could wait no longer, and the husband and wife heard her voice growing fainter and fainter as she left them.

"I am sure there is something wrong," the Mist Girl said, suddenly wide awake. "Listen, I can hear the forest birds singing."

They listened. Hine-wai had gone but the song of the birds was very loud and there were voices on the marae. Hine-pukohu-rangi ran to the door, forgetting her cloak. She opened it and the broad daylight flooded the whare. She stood there for a moment and a gasp of amazement went up from the people, for the Mist Girl was so slender and beautiful that no one had ever seen anything so wonderful before. She did not look as though she belonged to the earth.

Uenuku followed her out, smiling because everyone was envying him his wife. As he passed through the doorway, Hine sprang on to the roof of the house and climbed up to the ridge-pole. Her long hair covered her body.

The exclamations of the people were silenced as she began to sing. It was a sad song; there was pain in it, and longing, and love for Uenuku. Then a strange thing happened.

Out of a clear sky a tiny cloud drifted down. It wreathed itself round her, fold on fold, until she could no longer be seen. Only her voice could be heard coming from the tiny cloud. Then the song stopped and there was silence. The cloud drifted away from the roof. It rose upwards, higher and higher, until it seemed to dissolve in the bright sunshine which bathed the empty ridge-pole in a glow of golden light.

Uenuku was heartbroken. He could not meet the pitying eyes of his friends. His whare was cold and cheerless. Night after night he waited for the Mist Girl to return, but she never came back.

One day he left his home and set out on a long search for his wife. He met with many adventures and passed through strange countries but no one could tell him what had become of Hine-pukohu-rangi.

As his search went on, year after year, he grew old and bent and toothless, and at last, lonely and disappointed, he died in a distant country.

He had paid for his thoughtlessness and pride, and so the far gods of space took pity on him. They lifted his old body and changed him into a many-coloured rainbow and set him in the sky where everyone could see him.

Hine-pukohu-rangi still rises when the sun comes over the hills and warms the damp earth, while Uenuku, the shining rainbow, circles his lovely wife with a band of glowing colour.

9

Tinirau and the Whale

Before Hina-uri took her son Tuhuruhuru up to the heaven of Rehua, Tinirau, the father, made arrangements for him to be baptised by a famous tohunga from a distant pa. He sent his canoe to bring Kae, the tohunga, to the ceremony in state.

After the performance of the rites and incantations that were some day to make a bold and fearless warrior of the baby, Tinirau and Kae walked together on the beach. When they reached the rocks at the end, Tinirau stopped and in a loud voice shouted, "Tutunui!" Kae looked round in surprise for he could see no one. The beach was deserted, and the only footprints were those they had made as they walked together on the sand. He looked inland but there was no sign of life among the manuka trees. He looked out over the ocean, thinking there might be a fisherman somewhere in his canoe, but the canoes were all drawn up on the beach by the pa.

Then to his surprise he saw a big shapeless mass rising out of the water. It was a whale. The water rushed off its back like a waterfall and two spouts of hot vapour soared in the air and drifted lazily on the breeze. Kae had never seen a living whale so close before. To his amazement it came closer until its body was touching the rock on which the two men stood.

Tinirau cut a piece of flesh from the side of the monster. The whale rolled its tiny eyes at him, gave a sigh and then slid back into deep water.

Kae could hardly believe his eyes. Tinirau saw his look of astonishment and laughed.

"Have you never heard of my pet whale?" he asked. "That is Tutunui. He is a friend of mine. He takes me over the sea faster than any canoe. He has a great affection for me."

Kae scarcely knew what to say.

"But what did you cut the flesh for?"

"That you will see when we have taken it from the cooking oven, and you sink your teeth into it."

That night Kae tossed uneasily on his mat in the Strangers' House. He had eaten too heartily of the whale meat and could not sleep. As he lay awake he coveted Tinirau's whale.

When the time came for Kae to return to his own village, Tinirau had a canoe in readiness for him, but Kae was not satisfied.

"Tinirau," he said, "are you satisfied with the karakia I have recited over your son?"

"Surely," Tinirau replied.

"And do you feel that they will make him a great fighter?"

"Of that I am sure, too, my friend."

"But perhaps the tohunga of your own tribe could have done as well."

"No, no," said Tinirau quickly, for he did nct wish to offend Kae. "No, it is only Kae who is powerful and has the favour of the gods."

"Then I have a favour to ask of you."

"Speak."

"It is this. Call Tutunui and let him carry me back to my own place."

Tinirau was dismayed at Kae's suggestion. "But you would be much more comfortable in the canoe," he said. "It is a more fitting place for a great tohunga. And you do not know how to ride Tutunui."

Kae's face darkened. "Do you think I have no strength or wit?" he demanded. "Do you imagine I have no power to guide your whale? Have a care, Tinirau."

The chief knew it was dangerous to anger a tohunga. He hastened to make his peace with him. "I was only joking. He shall take you to your pa. But remember this, Kae. When you are near the shore, Tutunui will shake himself. That is a sign that he cannot go further in safety. When he gives the signal, jump off quickly from his right side and swim ashore."

"I know," Kae said impatiently.

Tinirau went down to the beach and lifted his hands to his mouth. "Tutunui!" he shouted, and in a few minutes they saw the whale coming close to the shore.

Kae scrambled on to his back and his strange voyage began. It did not take long, for Tutunui swam quickly. Kae soon became used to the sensation of riding on the back of a whale.

Before long they approached his pa. The whale shook himself to show Kae that it was time for him to jump off; but Kae took no notice. Tutunui shook himself again, but Kae pressed heavily on his back, repeating incantations, until Tutunui sank in the shallow water. He struggled, but Kae continued to weigh heavily on him while he sank in the soft sand. The tiny particles filled his blow-holes, and with a final flurry, Tutunui lay still and died.

There was great rejoicing in Kae's pa that night. The people were all there, and steam rose from the ovens where the flesh of Tutunui was cooking.

Far away on the Sacred Isle, Tinirau looked in vain for his whale to return. Always in the past his cry of "Tutunui!" had brought his pet to him. Tonight his voice boomed out over the water and was lost in the distance. Suddenly he raised his head, his nostrils distended in the evening breeze. From far-off Tihi-o-Manono, where Kae and his people lived, there came the delicious odour of cooked food.

Tinirau addressed his people while the moon made a silver path over the sea. "Kae has stolen my whale. Who will go with me to avenge this insult?"

The warriors leaped eagerly to their feet.

"We will go with you, Tinirau!" they shouted as one man.

"No," said a soft voice. "I will go, I, Hine-te-iwaiwa."*

The people looked at her in astonishment. "Yes, I will go, and other women of our tribe. Kae has many fighting men. Let the women go. We will bring him back to you without shedding of blood, O Tinirau, that you may avenge his insult to you."

In the house of Kae there was laughter. Hine-te-iwaiwa and many other women of Tinirau's tribe were there. They had travelled from village to village entertaining everyone with their songs and dances.

---

* The wife of Tinirau. Her other name was Hina-uri, and her story is told on page 75.

With a final flurry, Tutunui lay still and died.

No one knew who they were. Now the men and women of Kae's tribe had gathered to see them.

As they danced, Hine-te-iwaiwa and her friends looked sharply about them. Somewhere in this house was their enemy, Kae. They would know him when he laughed, for his teeth were broken and uneven.

The laughter of the people rang in the rafters of the house as the women played their games. Only one man sat with grim face, silent and close-lipped. The women had saved their best item until the last. Even the silent man was forced to laugh. When he put back his head and opened his mouth, everyone could see the ugly broken teeth. It was Kae.

When the fire had died down and all was quiet in the house, the women sang a soft song of magic which caused their hosts to sleep soundly. They crept to the door and arranged themselves in two long lines. They lifted Kae gently, wrapped his sleeping mats round him and carried him down to the beach and laid him in their canoe. Kae slept his enchanted sleep as they sped back to Motutapu, the Sacred Isle. The dawn had just brightened the sky as they picked up their living burden again and carried him to Tinirau's house, where they laid him upon his sleeping mat again.

It was broad daylight when Kae awoke. Tinirau walked up to his house, while the tribes-people called out, "Here comes Tinirau; it is Tinirau!"

The mists of sleep still hung about Kae's brain. He knew nothing of the night and fancied himself still in his own house. Tinirau walked up to the door and cried, "Greetings to you, O Kae!"

"Why have you come to my house?" asked Kae.

"Ah!" Tinirau said, "Why have you, O Kae, come to the house of Tinirau?"

"What do you mean? This is my house."

"Look about you, O Kae."

Kae looked round him. The house seemed different. The reed pattern on the walls was different. The carved posts were different. He looked out of the door, past Tinirau, and saw only the friendless, grinning faces of strangers.

Then he knew. He bowed his head.

The death of Tutunui, the whale, was avenged.

10

The Coming of the Maori

If you look at the map on the next page, you will notice a triangle of which New Zealand, the Hawaiian Islands and Easter Island make up the points. This is called the "Polynesian Triangle" because, on the hundreds of islands within its boundaries, live people of the same general appearance and with closely related languages – people who, like the New Zealand Maori, are tall and gracefully built, with light brown skins and dark, wavy hair, and who have similar customs and beliefs.

Who are these Polynesian folk, and whence did they come into the myriad islands of the Pacific? That is a question which scientists have been attempting to answer ever since the first white men came venturing into the Great Ocean of Kiwa. Perhaps there will never be any definite answer to this riddle, for the ancient forefathers of the Polynesians had no means of recording their history apart from passing it down from generation to generation by word of mouth. There are, however, certain clues which scientific men can use which tell us that the ancestors of the Polynesian peoples came from Southern Asia. We can be fairly certain that in earlier centuries they came from Eastern India to Southern Asia. It must have been thousands of years ago that these ancestors left their homeland, for the Polynesians knew nothing of the wheel, of metals, or of the art of pottery, all things which have been common knowledge in India and South-East Asia for countless years. Of course they may once have possessed this knowledge, only to lose it during their ages-long passage through Micronesia, for there exists no ore for extracting metals nor clay for pottery on these tiny isles and wheels would be of little practical use on the sandy beaches.

Once into the islands of Polynesia, it is believed that the

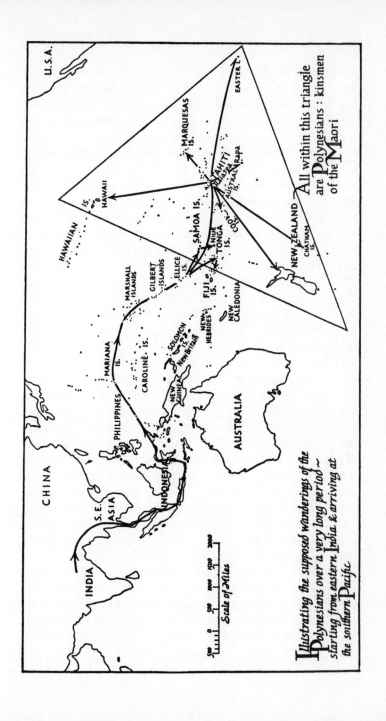

All within this triangle : kinsmen
are Polynesians of the Maori

U.S.A.

EASTER T.

MARQUESAS IS.

HAWAII
IS.

TAHITI
Rapa
AUSTRAL IS.

SAMOA IS.

NIUE
TONGA IS.

COOK IS.

NEW ZEALAND

CHATHAM IS.

HAWAIIAN

MARSHALL ISLANDS

GILBERT ISLANDS

ELLICE IS.

FIJI IS.

NEW CALEDONIA

MARIANA IS.

CAROLINE IS.

SOLOMON IS.
New Britain
NEW HEBRIDES

PHILIPPINES

CHINA

S.E. ASIA

INDONESIA

NEW GUINEA

AUSTRALIA

INDIA

Illustrating the supposed wanderings of the
Polynesians over a very long period —
starting from eastern India & arriving at
the southern Pacific

0   200   500   1000   1500   2000
Scale of Miles

Polynesians first populated two major centres – Samoa-Tonga in the west, and the Tahiti Group in the East. From these two great population centres radiated parties of colonists to the neighbouring islands. Samoa-Tonga colonised Niue, the Ellice Islands, the Tokelaus, Futuna and Uvea, and other smaller islands. The larger and more energetic Tahiti Group sent colonising parties (whether by design, or by accident of wind and current, we cannot say) across the watery miles to far Hawaii, to Rarotonga, the Marquesas, the Easter Island and Rapa, and to Aotearoa, which we know as New Zealand. From Hawaiki, which the Maori also called Rangiatea (the modern Tahitian Ra'iatea), they sailed to their new home.

Before we hear of their vast journeyings where ancient legend and story alone have given us history, we should try to picture the ocean-going canoes of the Vikings of the Sunrise. These canoes were of two kinds, single and double. In some cases they were over a hundred feet in length and were manned by a crew of one hundred and forty. The ones which came to New Zealand were either double canoes or ones with outriggers. Some of the double ones had a small house built on a platform connecting the two canoes. Sleeping accommodation was cramped, but as the work was divided into regular watches there was no need for sleeping space for the whole crew at once. The hollowed tree trunk which formed the canoe had its sides built up with many slabs joined neatly together, each plank being sewed to the next with sinnet which was passed through holes bored through raised edges on the inside of the planks. Thwarts lashed across the top-strakes stiffened the vessel and in bad weather splashboards were fitted. In heavy storms the canoes rode out the storm at a sea-anchor with a larger one at the stern to keep up the bow. Pointed six-foot paddles were also used, and with both paddle and sail the canoes quickly covered the long leagues of their epoch-making journeys.

There are little wisps of tradition giving a clue to the people who came to this land countless years ago, but we know less of them than of Maui who drew the land up from the home of Tangaroa. It was Kupe who first named the new land when it rose from the depths after many long days of voyaging, a thousand years ago. "He ao! He ao!" – "A cloud! A cloud!" cried his wife and as they sailed on the cloud grew before their eyes as a long bright world, the land

of the long-lingering daylight – Aotearoa! Kupe, in the canoe
Matahorua, and his companion Ngahue, in the Tahiri-rangi, made
their landfall in the far north. They sailed down the East Coast,
landing at places which we now know as Castle Point and Palliser
Bay, and into Wellington Harbour. Their camp-fire twinkled under
the karaka trees in the silent bush at Seatoun where now the sub-
urban traffic destroys the quietness of the night, and the headlights
of motorcars sweep along the waterfront.

Leaving Wellington, they sailed through the Strait to Porirua.
After a brief visit to the South Island they finally turned their
prows down (as the Maoris put it) to their own island home. They
sailed along the West Coast, finally leaving for Hokianga, "Kupe's
Returning Place," and across the rolling sea-wastes to Rarotonga,
and thence to their own people. They had a priceless gift for them
– a new land of peace and plenty with sailing directions for their
guidance.

Only this brief story of Kupe's deeds and place-names along the
coast of Aotearoa bears witness to the great adventure. But to the
fellow-tribesmen of Kupe and Ngahue the story of what they had
seen was enough. The forest was filled with many-hued birds.
There were no beasts of prey in that green and lovely land. There
was only the moa, the bird with a stature so great that in its sight
they were as grasshoppers. Yet even the moa was not to be feared.
In token of his prowess and as a witness that his story was true
Ngahue had brought back some of its flesh. One other thing
Ngahue brought with him – pounamu or greenstone which he had
found at Arahura. He broke off a piece of it and took it back with
him. From it were made a hei-tiki, an eardrop, and two axes which,
four centuries later, were used in the making of the canoes of the
Great Migration.

About thirty generations ago a canoe race was held in the lagoon
of Pikopiko-i-whiti in Hawaiki. The old chief, Toi, and other elders
of the tribe sat on the slopes of a hill to watch the race. The victors
were two young men named Whatonga and Tu Rahui. In the pride
of their youth they sailed out of the harbour and into the open sea.
Before they could return a sudden storm arose and swept them out
of sight. Toi was smitten with grief. Whatonga was his grandson,

and day after day he kept watch for the return of the canoes, but in vain. When several moons had passed, and it seemed hopeless to watch for the returning sails, Toil prepared himself to set out in search of his grandson in the canoe Te Paepae-ki-Rarotonga. He reached Pangopango (in the Samoan group) where some of the missing people were found, but Whatonga was not among them.

The old warrior set out for the far-distant country which Kupe had visited so many years before. He called at Rarotonga on his way and then set sail for the southern seas. Missing his objective, he made the Chatham Islands where he stayed for a time. Sails were set once again , and he arrived at Aotearoa, landing at Tamaki. His search for his grandson had proved fruitless, and at last the old man, wearied and disheartened by his long voyaging, decided to settle in the new country. He made his home at Whakatane, far from his own people, his only neighbours being the tangata-whenua (the people of the land, the original inhabitants). Instead of the kumara and other foods he was accustomed to, he had to depend on the products of the forest and on fern root, varied only by dishes of fish and fowl. It was here he earned his name, Toi-kai-rakau – Toi the Wood-eater.

In the meantime Whatonga had arrived at Rangiatea (Ra'iatea). He found his way home again, only to learn that his grandfather had left in search of him. He determined to find Toi, and in the canoe Kurahaupo he set sail with a crew of sixty men and several women. He landed at Tongaporutu and there he heard of Toi-kai-rakau who lived at Whakatane on the other side of the island, so he sailed north again, rounded the North Cape, and landed at Maketu. With great rejoicing Toi greeted his grandson in a pa maioro (a village with earthwork defences) called Kapu-te-rangi, on a hill overlooking the present Whakatane. There, after so long a separation, grandfather and grandson were at last united.

Eventually Whatonga moved to Mahia, and in his old age his two tons, Tara and Tautoki, settled at Wellington Harbour, which was named Te Whanga-nui-a-Tara – The Great Harbour of Tara.

While Whatonga was searching for his grandfather, two chiefs in Hawaiki named Nuku and Manaia were at war. Manaia, being the weaker of the two, made his escape in the Tokomaru canoe. Nuku and his people pursued the vanquished chief in the three canoes Te Houama, Waimate and Tangi-apakura. Both Manaia and Nuku touched at Rarotonga and then came on to Aotearoa. Manaia passed through the Straits and landed at Rangitoto (D'Urville Island). When Nuku arrived, Manaia had gone, but the ashes of his camp-fire were still warm. The chase continued until Manaia was sighted at Pukerua, a few miles from Wellington. A terrible fight ensued until darkness fell, and then friendly night hid the warriors from sight. The two chiefs then agreed to land in peace and take up arms against each other the next day. They went ashore at Paekakariki, but all that night a fierce gale blew and the heavy ocean rollers thundered on the shore. This storm was caused by the magic of Manaia. The gale was so fierce that it formed all the sand-dunes from Paekakariki to Otaki. The fighting strength of Nuku was broken by the storm, so peace was declared and he returned to Hawaiki, but Manaia remained in Aotearoa.

For the next two hundred years many crossings and recrossings of the southern seas were made. Little is known of these voyages. They are but dim memories of the shadowed past.

It is from the Great Migration of the fourteenth century that the Maori loves to trace his descent. It was the last of his long voyages – the final brilliant light before the torch guttered out. Then Aotearoa became a different world, cut off from other lands which were kept alive in the memories of men only by the old-time tales and the names of the fatherland which were given to places in many parts of Aotearoa to remind the Maori of his loved Hawaiki.

Fierce wars had broken out in the tropic islands. Over-population and shortage of food were the principal cause. For these and other reasons a brave company of people set sail over the trackless ocean in their picturesquely named canoes – Arawa (Shark), Tainui (Great Tide), Mata-atua (Face of a God), Kura-haupo (Storm Cloud), and Tokomaru (Shade of the South). In addition there were the Aotea, Takitimu and Horouta which sailed about the same time, and are usually included in the fleet.

The grey rollers of the Ocean of Kiwa beckoned the hardy seafarers. The canoes moved restlessly as the triangular sails were hoisted, and cries of lamentation and farewell rose above the

The fleet sets out from Hawaiki.

sighing of the trade winds in the palms. It was farewell, farewell to Hawaiki the Golden, to days in the hot summer sun, to laughter and song and happy memories of the palm-fringed shores of their native land. But it was also farewell to Tu, the War God, who stalked in their midst, whose shadow lay over them. It was farewell to the tropic sun which could not ripen enough fruit to satisfy their hunger.

A sudden hush had fallen. Where the white wavelets lapped the sand stood the grey-haired patriarch, Hou-mai-tawhiti. His voice was lifted up in the poroporoaki, the farewell: "Follow not after the god of War in your country of the south; hold to the deeds of Rongo the Peaceful. Haere! Haere! Haere atu ra."

His voice died away into silence; the wind bore away the soft refrain; the waves caressed the canoes as they slid away from the shore. Te Arawa led the way, her three sails carrying her swiftly out into the ocean. The other canoes followed, fading one by one into the distance, frail-winged birds that dared the perils of the open sea.

The Arawa was first of them all; Tama-te-kapua, Son of the Clouds, the son of Hou-mai-tawhiti, was her captain. He chuckled to himself as the Arawa lifted to the long waves of the ocean. Before leaving he had asked Ngatoro, the famous tohunga, to come aboard to perform the sacred rites which would ensure the protection of the atua and the ancestral spirits. Ngatoro had come unsuspecting, bringing Kearoa, his wife, with him. As soon as they had set foot in the canoe, Tama-te-Kapua had ordered the sails to be raised, and before the tohunga and his wife could protest, they were sailing beyond the reach of the other canoes. This was the reason why the Arawa led the other canoes out of the harbour.

Ngatoro was furious, but Tama pacified him by telling him that his own canoe would follow quickly and that he would hold Te Arawa back until the other canoes caught up with it. But as the Arawa lifted her head to the waves and the rigging sang in the breeze, Ngatoro realised that Tama's words were empty and that he and his wife would have to remain where they were for the whole of the long voyage. By keeping them with him, Tama hoped to win the favour of the gods, for Ngatoro was wise in their ways. The tohunga said nothing, but in his heart he planned revenge.

Te Arawa in the grip of Korokoro-o-te-Parata,
the throat of the sea-monster.

In Hawaiki, now far distant from the canoes, incantations to the gods rose each day like smoke in the still air of morning for the confounding of Tama from another whom he had wronged – prayers that changed the stars of the morning to those of the evening, and of evening to morning.

One day, Ngatoro climbed to the roof of the house built on the platform connecting the two canoes, and called aloud to the heavens. His power went out in waves from the lonely vessel and great winds sprang to life from a clear sky. The canoe turned its prow towards Korokoro-o-te-Parata, the throat of the sea-monster, to the steep descent where the world ends. The waves licked round the Arawa, the sky grew dull and heavy, and the canoe was drawn into the outer spirals of the maelstrom. The carved prow disappeared, the water reached the first bailing place, the second in the middle of the canoe. From his place on the house Ngatoro heard the gods splashing in the water and saw the crew grasping the thwarts to save themselves from being thrown out. There was no expression on his carved face, but as one after another of the crew lost his hold on the slippery boards and was drawn into the racing water, he took pity on them and invoked the protection of Tangaroa, god of the sea.

There was no hint of fear in Tama's eyes. He looked calmly at the boiling water as if calculating their chance of escape. A storm-assuaging incantation came from Ngatoro's lips. He called upon the spirits of Ruarangi and of Maui to "clear from perils all the ocean track of Ngatoro," and gradually the white throat of Parata closed and the boiling waters calmed down.

There were many leagues still to be sailed. Day after day passed by and every evening the sun was engulfed in the endless sea. Then the lonely sails were rocked in the black void and only the sound of the waves, the creaking of cordage and the sough of the wind came to the ears of the seafarers. The rising moon shone over the empty wastes and only the black shape of a following fin broke the silvered surface.

After many days the new land came in sight. As they glided into the harbour the water was like glass, reflecting the blazing glory of the flowering pohutukawa. Vivid crimson flamed onshore and in the water, putting to shame the bright colour of their head ornaments. Immediately the distant glory of the pohutukawa was seen,

Landfall for Te Arawa.

one of the men threw his red head ornaments into the sea, calling out, "See there, red ornaments for the head are more plentiful in this country than in Hawaiki. I throw my red head ornament into the water." He and the other chiefs were bitterly disappointed when they found that the glowing colour came only from the flowers which withered as soon as they were placed in the hair and crumbled at a touch. The kura or head ornaments of Hawaiki were made from the red feathers of a bird and worn only by the highest chiefs.

Most of the canoes of the migration arrived about this time, and disputes rose between them as to who were the first arrivals. A whale was stranded on the beach and the captain of each canoe claimed it as his own. It was on this account that the bay received its name – Whangaparaoa, the Bay of the Sperm Whale. The captains tried to decide matters in a friendly fashion. Sacred places had been set up on shore by the different canoes. When they were examined it was found that the posts set up by the people of Tainui were withered and dried, whilst those of the other canoes were fresh and green. The Tainui, therefore, claimed the whale and the honour of being the first arrival.

The Arawa people planted the kumara at Whangaparaoa, and there it grows to this day. Shortly afterwards this canoe separated from the others. One hundred and forty men under the chief Taikehu explored the north-west coastline. The Arawa then sailed to Motiti, which was named after a place in Hawaiki on account of the shortage of firewood there, and later to Maketu. There the people set up their altar which they named in remembrance of their ancient home. There are rocks at Maketu which are pointed out as the bow and stern anchors of the Arawa. The stern anchor, Tu-te-rangi-haruru, is a solid outcrop to which the stern-line was probably tied. The descendants of Tama peopled the Hot Lakes region, those of Ngatoro, Lake Taupo, and so it is said of the Arawa canoe that the bowpiece is Maketu and the sternpiece Tongariro.

Ngatoro travelled about the country, and when he found dry valleys he stamped on the earth and brought forth springs of water. He visited the mountains and peopled them with patu-paiarehe (fairies). He was making up for lost time, for when the Arawa was beached at Maketu, his duties as tohunga prevented him from selecting land for himself while the other chiefs made their choice. He feared that all the best land might be taken, but his slave told him of a high snow-capped mountain from the summit of which, if he could only reach it, he might survey a large part of the island and thus secure a larger share of the land than the other chiefs.

Ngatoro saw the wisdom of his slave's suggestion. As soon as his duties were over he set off in company with the slave and a favourite dog for the summit of Mount Tongariro. They struggled up the steep sides and at last stood on the summit, their breath going up like steam in the cold air. As Ngatoro looked round him he claimed all the land he could see for himself and his descendants, but in order to establish a claim he had to give names to every hill and valley and forest.

Unhesitatingly he named them, some of them after the places he remembered in his homeland, others on account of their appearance, or of some incident that had happened as he travelled over them. He came to the end. He looked down and saw his slave lying stiff and cold on the snow. He had frozen to death on the cold mountain peak. As he bent over him, Ngatoro felt his own limbs growing stiff. It was an effort to breathe in the thin air and the cold cut him like a knife. He moved over to his dog and clutched the thick fur, and bade it carry him down the mountain. The dog struggled to its feet and began to crawl down the mountain side, dragging its master with it, but gradually its steps grew slower. Ngatoro urged it on, but at last the dog fell to the ground, frozen to death. The tohunga felt the icy numbness that comes before death. It was creeping up his body.

Knowing that he would never be able to get down to the warmer lowlands unaided, Ngatoro called upon his sisters in far-off Hawaiki to come to his aid. Across the sea of Kiwa they heard their brother's voice, and snatching a blazing brand from the sacred fire, they plunged into the sea. They swam under the water until they reached the Bay of Plenty, where they came to the surface to find out where they were. The water caught fire as they looked about them, and has continued to burn ever since on the spot known to us as White Island. They dived again, and their underground course is marked by the hot springs of the Rotorua and Taupo districts. Finally they reached Tongariro and with the warmth of their bodies they brought Ngatoro back to the life that was slipping away from him.

Back at Maketu, Tama was dissatisfied and restless. He went further north to Tauranga, where he found Taikehu, but his restless spirit drove him on to Moehau and Hauraki. It was at Cape Colville that he finally made his home, and there he died. Ngatoro and his wife had taken up their abode on Motiti Island, but Tama-te-Kapua was buried by his sons on the forested ridge of Moehau. He was left in peace there, for his relatives went back to Maketu.

His sons said of him, when they buried him:

"Let him slumber here where his spirit can gaze far over the ocean and over the land of Aotearoa. And the winds that sweep across the great ocean of Kiwa, they shall ever sing his oriori, his wild lullaby."

It was a fitting funeral song for the famous sailor. His memorial is the name the Maori has for the cape:

> *Te-Moe-hau-o-Tama-te-Kapua,*
> *Tama's Windy Sleeping Place.*

The Tainui canoe was built after the Arawa. Her history is intertwined with that of the Arawa, for there was bitterness of feeling between the men of the two canoes after Tama-te-Kapua's treachery in abducting Ngaroro-i-rangi and his wife. The Tainui, like the Arawa, was a double canoe, and Hoturoa was her captain. After leaving Whangaparaoa, the Tainui came to Tamaki, where the seafarers landed. They went up the river till they came to the portage. There they saw seagulls and oyster-catchers flying overhead from the west and surmised that the ocean on the other side of the land could not be far away. In the distance they saw the silvery gleam of the Manukau, and they determined to drag the canoe overland at Otahuhu and launch her again.

Other canoes had come to Tamaki. The Tokomaru crossed the island first, but the Tainui soon followed, and sailed into the peaceful waters of the Manukau. At Wai-whaka-ruku-rupu-hanga, between the rivers Waihou and Piako, the anchor stone of the Tainui can still be seen. It is a large stone known to tradition as Te Pungapunga. The canoe finally reached Kawhia where it was beached and later buried. The head and stern pieces, turned to stone, can be seen projecting above the ground to this day. The Arawa canoe was burnt by Raumati, of the Tainui tribe, thus causing endless strife between the two peoples. The descendants of Tainui settled in the Waikato.

The Mata-atua canoe was made, it is said, of one half of a tree that fell and split into two pieces, and was made into two canoes. Toroa was her captain and her final resting place, Whakatane.

The Tokomaru rounded the North Cape and came down to the West Coast as far as the Mohakatino River in Taranaki.

Little is known of the Kura-haupo canoe. The Nga-Puhi of the North say it was petrified into a reef on the East Coast, but the Aotea people say it was wrecked and the occupants transferred to their own canoe.

Of the canoes which did not accompany the Great Fleet but sailed about the same time, the Aotea, commanded by Turi, sailed from Ra-iatea but did not call at Rarotonga. Instead she was beached at Rangi-tahua (Sunday Island) where she was refitted and a dog killed to propitiate Maru. Ririno also sailed with Aotea, but they quarrelled over Kupe's sailing direction and parted company. Some say that the Ririno was lost, others that it was wrecked on Boulder Bank, near Nelson.

The Aotea gave its name to a small harbour on the West Coast where the crew first landed. She was abandoned there, Turi and his men following the coastline by land until they reached the Patea River, where they settled. Their descendants made their way up the Whanganui River. It is said that Turi brought many valuable plants with him.

Five canoes left Hawaiki under Tamatea, but only two survived – the Takitimu and Horouta. A careful choice was made and only the strongest men and women selected for the journey, yet so great were the hazards of the voyage that three of the canoes were lost on the way.

On account of her speed, and with the help of the tohunga who called upon the gods of the sea for assistance, the Takitimu was the first arrival. She landed near the North Cape, but a heavy storm arose, and she put to sea again. After rounding the North Cape she sailed on to Whakatane. A pa was built and a number of the crew settled there. Tamatea took the canoe back to the Bay of Islands where about one quarter of his followers were left. Setting out again, he came to Waiapu where he found others who had sailed in the Horouta. Still more of his people were left at Waiapu, but the restless Tamatea pushed off and visited the South Island, staying awhile and then journeying northwards to Whanganui, ascending the river, and travelling over to Taupo and Whakatane. Another tradition says that the Takitimu was petrified into a range of mountains in Otago.

So the country was settled. Descendants of the Arawa and Mata-atua voyagers settled in different parts of the Bay of Plenty, those of Tainui in the Waikato, those of the Aotea in Taranaki; while the descendants of the pioneering Takitimu and Horouta sailors are to be found in the East Coast and East Cape districts, Aotearoa thus being roughly divided into canoe districts.

There were other canoes. Some of the names have come to us by the paths and byways of legend, but we know little of them save this: that the great deeds of these early voyagers were no isolated acts of bravery. In those days the seas were but highways to the hardy southern mariners. There are records of crossings and re-crossings of the stormy seas, and the bringing of food and other supplies to the pioneers.

And then, isolation. For many generations there were none who dared pass the Throat of the Sea Monster until at length the great white bird with the pale-skinned mariners sailed into these forgotten seas, heralding the advent of the Pakeha to the Land of the Maori.

This is the story of the coming of the Maori. It is history, but history that has come to us through the unwritten pages of ancient legend and story.

11

Wooden Head

Hear now the story of the magical wooden head of the Sacred Mountain.

Puarata was a powerful magician who owned a wooden head which stared across the sea with sightless eyes. This image was the home of the evil spirits of the tohunga. The Sacred Mountain was feared by everyone, and throughout Te Ika a Maui men spoke in hushed tones when the wooden head was mentioned. It was death to pass near the Sacred Mountain, for Puarata seemed to smell out strangers in his country. Then he would whisper to the wooden head and a terrible cry would rise from its evil spirit. It rang through the forest and across the plains and no living thing could bear to hear that cry.

As the years went by the land round about grew deserted and silent, for there were no birds in the forest and the hardy traveller who ventured too near would see the whitened bones of those who had heard the voice of the head and who had died as they listened.

Stories of this evil magic reached the ears of Hakawau, a powerful priest whose spirit hated evil. Sometimes he lay awake at night while the call of a morepork reminded him of the evil cry that came from Puarata's pa. It seemed to him then that some day he would be called on to do battle with those evil powers.

One night he called the spirits to him and fell into an enchanted sleep. While he slept he seemed to see his own spirit standing before him. As he watched it began to grow and grow until its head touched the clouds. When he awoke Hakawau felt full of confidence for he knew that his spirit was powerful and he believed that it would overcome the wooden head of Puarata.

Without waiting any longer he set off towards the Sacred Mountain with a friend. They travelled swiftly across country, pausing only to eat the food they had brought with them. When anyone

The bones lay in drifts like snow
among the trees.

stopped them and asked them to eat, Hakawau said, "We must hurry, for our task is urgent. We have eaten already." Presently they came to Waitara. Hakawau's companion became fearful for even at this distance the wooden head had been known to kill.

"Do not be afraid," Hakawau said, and broke into a chant that cheered his friend.

Then they came to Te Weta.

"I am frightened," said Hakawau's friend. "I can hear my heart beating. Look, there are white bones among the trees."

"The time for being afraid has not come yet," Hakawau replied scornfully.

When they came to Waimatuku even Hakawau went cautiously, for the bones lay in drifts like snow among the trees.

He repeated his spells and the two men went on, putting each foot forward with caution, for who could tell when death might not strike unseen. They went along the paths slowly and up a low hill. On the crest they lay down and looked through the fern. The Sacred Mountain with the pa on its summit was straight in front of them. They saw people moving behind the palisades and sentries walking up and down, but no one noticed the two travellers who were spying out the land.

There were no bones amongst the ferns that spread across the valley and lifted themselves up towards the pa, which seemed to grow out of the mountain. Never before had anyone come so close to the Sacred Mountain unharmed.

"Now I am not afraid," Hakawau's companion said. "Now I can see that these are men such as ourselves. Here is something we can fight."

"It is now that we must be careful," Hakawau warned him. "The evil spirits of Puarata are swarming round us though we cannot see them. Keep quiet for I must call up my own spirits. You will not see anything, and you must not speak."

The man looked astonished, for Hakawau was staring in front of him with sightless eyes. The people still walked about the fortress. The smoke of the cooking fires spiralled up in the quiet air. The sentries still stood on their platforms. A low muttering came from Hakawau's lips and he seemed to be giving orders. His eyes were not sightless, for he could see Puarata's evil spirits clustered thickly behind the palisades. His own pressed round him like fighting men.

"Go down into the valley and challenge them," he said to some.

They rushed down the valley like a wave and began to climb the hill towards the pa. Presently the attackers were thrown back. Some of them began to run down the hillside, then others followed until they were all in full retreat. Puarata's spirits leaped about in silent frenzy. They could not resist the sight of their defeated enemy flying from them. They swarmed through the palisades and rushed after them. Right into the hollows of the valley they went. Not one was left in the pa.

Hakawau's spirits were hiding in the fern and those of Puarata passed them. Presently they looked back and saw another band of Hakawau's spirits coming over the shoulder of the spur behind them and climbing up towards the pa. The attackers had outwitted them. They rushed up the hill again, but as soon as their backs were turned, the spirits that had been hiding in the fern leaped upon them and killed them. Only a few of them reached the pa, and there they fell before the weapons of the enemy spirits which had already clustered there.

"Aa!" said Hakawau, and shuddered. "It is over. They are beaten."

His companion looked at him in amazement. "How can you say they are beaten?" he asked. 'Nothing has happened. The sentries have not even seen us. Nothing is changed."

"Puarata is empty," Hakawau replied. "Puarata is an empty canoe. Once he carried evil spirits inside him and sent them out to do his will. Today they went out at his bidding, but they have all been destroyed and Puarata is empty. Let us go forward."

They stood up, and at once the sentries shouted the alarm. They were amazed to see anyone alive so close to their pa. With every step the travellers took they expected them to fall, but still they advanced.

"Puarata!" the sentries called, "Puarata, strangers are coming!"

They had no fight in them; they were all like old women because Puarata's spirits had been their warriors.

Puarata felt his emptiness. He hurried to the wooden head and cried, "Strangers are coming1 Two mighty warriors!" but the wooden head had lost its power. Instead of the cry that used to come from its lips, petrifying travellers many miles away at Te Weta and even at Waitara, there was only a thin wailing like that of a baby.

When the two warriors had nearly reached the pa, Hakawau said to his companion, "Go straight along the path and through the gateway into the pa. As for me, I will show my power by going over the parapet."

As he climbed the wooden stakes the people shouted angrily, "Get down and go through the gateway as your friend is doing."

Hakawau took no notice. He jumped down from the fence and entered the sacred places of the pa. The wooden head was silent. It had lost its power and was nothing but a carved block of wood.

Puarata watched the tohunga from under lowered brows but dared not say anything. Presently Hakawau and his companion lay down and rested to show their contempt for the magicians of the Sacred Mountain and their wooden head.

The people dared not touch them for they had met a magic stronger than their own.

Puarata was nowhere to be seen. Presently they heard him calling to some of his people and Hakawau smiled grimly.

When they were rested, Hakawau stood up and called his friend to come with him. Some of the people came up and begged them to eat before they left. An appetising smell came from the flax food baskets.

"We ate only a little while ago," Hakawau replied. "We are not hungry."

They continued to press food on him, smiling and pretending to be anxious for his welfare.

"You should not have listened to Puarata," Hakawau said sternly. "He was full of evil spirits. Great wrong was done here. For this reason we came, that the cry of the wooden head should no longer beat into men's brains and kill them. I have emptied evil out of Puarata, but now I see that some of it has come back. Had we eaten this food, we should not have lived. Aue! Alas, now it is you who will die."

He struck the door of the house where he had rested and went out through the gate with his companion.

They did not look back until they had crossed the valley and reached the ridge where they had lain during the battle of the spirits.

The smoke from the cooking fires was the only thing that moved. Wooden head was silent, and Puarata and all his people were dead. And from that day to this, men have passed the Sacred Mountain without any fear of the cry that comes through wooden lips and tears through the tissues of the brain.

12

Ponga and Puhihuia

There was continual warfare between the Tainui people on Maungawhau (Mount Eden) and those who lived at Awhitu on the Manukau Harbour. The people of Awhitu maintained that the shark fishing ground at Puponga was theirs, but those of Maungawhau claimed the favoured spot for themselves. This led to warfare and many people were killed; but because they were all of Tainui some of the elders were concerned, and they made peace with each other – until someone went fishing, and then the trouble started all over again.

During a time of peace, the people of Maungawhau went to visit their friends at Awhitu. Among them was a beautiful girl whose name was Puhihuia, while among the lesser chiefs of Awhitu was a young warrior named Ponga. He fell in love with Puhihuia as soon as he saw her, but he was not the only one among the young chiefs who noticed the beautiful girl of Maungawhau.

Some time afterwards the people of Awhitu visited their relatives at Maungawhau. The young men prepared presents for the girls, gathering the ripe fruit of the miro to make sweet oil, and herbs and grasses for scent. Most of them had brothers and sisters to help them, but Ponga was an only son. He asked his mother how to procure the scented oil, and she and her friends made some for him.

At last the day came when the young men of Awhitu were able to visit Maungawhau and take part in the hakas and the games. There were many people on the marae, and the dancers stood ready in their ranks. First came the steady stamping of the young men of Maungawhau. Puhihuia was looking on, ready to take her part. At the right moment she dashed forward with glaring eyes and protruding tongue, contorting her face and body in the dance that welcomed the visitors. Ponga's heart almost suffocated him with its rapid beating as he watched her, but he said nothing to his friends, all of whom were overcome with admiration for the girl.

When the people of Awhitu danced their haka, Ponga was the leader. When the dancing was over, Ponga went back with the other young men to the guest house. He could not sleep. After turning restlessly from side to side, he went outside, followed by his slave, who sat with him in the darkness.

"Perhaps you are weary. You must have over-exerted yourself in the haka," the slave said. "Herring-fishers sleep while eel-fishers rise up."

"This is not my own home," Ponga replied. "I am thinking of other things."

The slave drew closer to him and whispered, "It is for the great ones of our party to grasp the sacredness of the pa."

Ponga looked at him closely. "Do you mean Puhihuia?"

"Yes. Did I not see how everyone's eyes flashed and glistened when Puhihuia was dancing before us, and yours most of all?"

"Friend, you are right. Let us go home. Our leaders have fallen in love with this lady, but if I took her for myself they would kill me."

Master and slave sat for a long time, thinking. At length the slave whispered again to his master. It was a plan that concerned the high-born girl of Maungawhau, and Ponga's eyes brightened.

The next night the rangatiras of both tribes sat talking together about the famous deeds of their ancestors. When the fires died down the old men went off to their own houses, but Ponga remained where he was. When everyone was asleep he called out to his slave to bring him some water. His voice carried clearly, and the mother of Puhihuia heard the request.

"Girl, are you deaf?" she said to her daughter. "Do you not hear the visitor calling to his slave? Go and get him some water."

The girl replied, "With the evil spirits of the night as thick as grass, I would be afraid," but she took a calabash and went outside. Ponga was looking out of the door and saw the girl in the distance.

"Let me go and find that obstinate slave of mine, for I am faint with thirst," he said, and hurried outside. He saw the light of Puhihuia's torch and her voice as she sang to encourage herself and keep the spirits away. He caught up with her at the spring and said,

"It is true that I thirst. But the thirst is of the heart. It is inside me, and I bring that thirst to you to be satisfied." Then the two young people knew that they had lost their hearts to each, but that their tribes would not permit them to proclaim their love.

The visitors were ready to return home. Before the sun rose Ponga sent his slave to Onehunga to cut the lashings of the topsides of the Maungawhau canoes, and to launch all the Awhitu canoes and keep them afloat.

When the morning meal was finished, the visitors took their departure. Gifts were exchanged as a sign of peace, and the young people of the Maungawhau pa accompanied their friends on the first part of the journey. Puhihuia went with them, but when her father saw her he shouted, "Girl, come back, come back! You are foolish to go too far. Come back, all of you." Her companions turned back at once, but Puhihuia started to run, gently at first, but faster and faster as she reached the plain. She caught up with Ponga. They joined hands and ran like feathers driven by the wind, or the woodhen escaped from the snare. The rangatiras of Maungawhau rushed fiercely after them.

Ponga and Puhihuia reached the canoes and set off down the harbour. The men of Maungawhau were not far behind them, but when they grasped the canoes to launch them, the top-pieces broke off and the haulers were hurled in all directions. Seeing that their visitors had made their escape, some of the men of Maungawhau stood on the beach and shouted, "Go on! Go on! But we will follow you. The sun shines, the sun sets, but we remain!"

The canoe in which Ponga and Puhihuia were seated reached the pa at Awhitu. When they saw the famous young woman of Maungawhau, those who had stayed at home came down to the water's edge to greet her, but the steersman of the canoe warned them of the trouble that was coming.

"Ponga has done us great harm," he said. 'His heart has been evil towards us. He has stolen the fair one of the Maungawhau, and our relatives will revenge themselves on us. Those who are brave must be brave, for if we are weak we shall be exterminated like the moa."

The chief of Awhitu stood up and said, "Carry the girl back to her home. I am not willing that the peace between us should be broken for the sake of a foolish boy."

Puhihuia leapt to her feet and waved her hand to the people on shore. She took off one of her outer garments and laid it at the feet of Ponga, standing before them in her fine white flaxen inner garment, bound with a girdle of karetu. She rolled this down from her shoulders and girded it round her waist. Stretching out her arms to the people, she said, "Look at me. You are wrong in blaming Ponga. I came here of my own accord; yours is the wrong. Look at the excellence of the young man Ponga. Why did you not keep him in your own place, and not let him come to my pa? If you had let his friends come without him I would now be on my own marae. It is you who are to blame – you who allowed the delight of my heart to come to me."

Her words melted the frozen heart of the chief and many of his people, and she was taken ashore as an honoured guest.

"The shining cuckoo has come into our midst," they said. "Its song is, 'Shine, life!', but unless we take care, it will be death that follows."

In the discussion that ensued there were some who gladly received the shining cuckoo of Maungawhau, but others dreaded the vengeance that would be taken by her tribesmen. They urged that she be sent back, and that Ponga be sacrificed for his presumption. Puhihuia spoke again at the chief's invitation.

"This wrong is not to be blamed on Ponga. It is your own, for you allowed him to come to my father's pa. Now that you have shown me what he is, I have chosen him for myself. Am I the first woman who has flown to the man of her choice? Although I am a woman, if the taua you are talking about comes here I will meet it with grimaces of defiance, even if Ponga and I have to meet it alone while you sit silent. What shall I do? Shall I return? Never! Never! I can at least travel with Ponga to the world of spirits."

Before they went to sleep, the men said, "The words of our chief are right. The lady is in love with Ponga. That is well. Let us help them. Let us be brave."

A careful watch was kept, and soon a canoe was seen approaching with a full crew. The chief fighting men gathered outside the pa. The canoe came close, and a rangatira demanded that Puhihuia should be returned to them. He was answered with defiant words, and Puhihuia told her people that nothing would turn her away from her lover. She bade her people, as they loved her, to come to her wedding feast. But no answer was given, and the canoe returned in silence.

At Maungawhau the discussion was tossed backwards and forwards all night. Some were angry and wished to destroy their friends at Awhitu, and to put Ponga and Puhihuia to death. It was not until the sky had paled in the light of the early dawn that the oldest tohunga summed up the feelings of most of the people.

"Puhihuia has bidden us to her marriage feast," he said. "Have we taken a dislike to shark's flesh as a relish with our summer kumara? We must send messages to Puhihuia and her friends to say that on the third day after the full moon we will arrive at Awhitu to answer her summons."

Puhihuia's mother did not agree. She said to the women of the pa, "This is our day. To Awhitu, to Awhitu! The men are not in this!" About sixty women answered her call, and arrayed themselves as warriors. They went to Onehunga, launched the canoes, and paddled on until they reached Awhitu. The mother of Puhihuia called out to the people of the pa, "Grasp your weapons, for we are a war party!"

The women of Maungawhau had paddled as men, their garments were girded round their waists, and they had plumes in their hair. No wonder that the people of Awhitu were deceived. Ponga and Puhihuia went to a cliff which overlooked the beach. The young woman recognised her mother and her friends.

"The paddlers are all women," she said, "but it may be that men are lying in the bilge. I will not be taken. I would rather leap from this cliff to my death."

Puhihuia's mother called out loudly, "Come outside, men of Awhitu. Why have you stolen my daughter? What have I taken from you that you should steal the pendant from my breast? Come outside, that we may fight."

The people remained silent. It was Puhihuia who took up the challenge.

"If I am killed," she said, "you can take my body away, but if I overcome your champion, you must return to your pa for the tangi. I will not return with you alive."

Some of the young women threw aside their outer garments and jumped into the water and swam ashore. They went to the foot of the cliff, while Puhihuia and Ponga descended to meet them. The young man tried to restrain her, and attempted to persuade her to run away with him, fearing for her safety. Puhihuia refused. She tucked her garment round her waist and went forward, holding her taiaha at the ready. One of the company of girls rose to meet her, holding a whalebone mere. She struck a blow at Puhihuia's head, but it was deftly parried. Puhihuia gave her antagonist a violent blow in the stomach, which put her out of action.

Another girl thrust at her with a short spear. Puhihuia leaped to one side and gave her a heavy blow on the shoulder which made her drop her weapon and retire from the contest. The next girl had a broad-bladed weapon. Her blow was parried, but not so well as the others, for the weapon struck the fringe of Puhihuia's garment. The girl struck again at Puhihuia, but this time the parry was successful, and with the same action a smart turn of the taiaha brought the tongue of the weapon violently against the girl's stomach. She collapsed, and rolled over on the sand. One after another the girls sprang forward, but each in turn was disarmed by Puhihuia. At length her mother stood up in the canoe and called out, "Girl, that is enough. You have defeated my warriors. Let us two now return to your father."

She replied scornfully, "Will Kupe return?"

"Enough, then. Remain here. I will go back and come again at the time of the marriage feast."

Hurried preparations were made for the great feast; fish were netted, fern-root was dug and stacked in heaps to dry, sharks were caught and hung on the stages, pigeons speared, pipis collected, cooked and hung on strings to dry, korau was cut and stored, the roots of fern-trees were steamed in the ovens, and paua were obtained from the rocks and steamed until they were cooked. On the appointed day a messenger was sent to Maungawhau to say that the feast was ready.

At last came the great day of the feast. The people of Maungawhau were entertained with dances and speeches of welcome. The rangatiras of Awhitu went to a long heap of treasures piled up on

Puhihuia gave her opponent
a heavy blow on the shoulder.

the marae. There were huia and albatross feathers, flax garments, greenstone, and many other prized possessions.

"These treasures," he said, "are for the parents of Puhihuia."

When he had finished the visitors brought their gifts of eels, hapuku, mackerel, dogs, preserved rats, dried pipis, potted kakas and kuakas and many other foods, and placed them in rows. They added garments, weapons, and bread made of hinau berries and raupo pollen. When all was ready, Puhihuia's father stood up and touched the gifts with his staff, saying, "O all you powers of darkness, all you powers of light, here are your treasures. O you gods and you ancient ones, and you children of Hotunui, here are your treasures. O my daughter, these treasures are for you. You are leaving me. I grieve for you. Go, my treasure, but you are not dead. We are descended from the same canoe. Farewell!"

The courage of the young woman who had followed her lover through every danger was then rewarded, and Ponga and Puhihuia lived together in peace and happiness at Awhitu.

13

Young Hatupatu

The story of Hatupatu is a tale which might well have been taken straight from the pages of the brothers Grimm. Hatupatu and his brothers lived somewhere between Rotorua and Taupo where the weird subterranean fires are forever creeping under the earth, appearing through the cracks in the rocks and heating the mud pools. Hatupatu's brothers spent most of their time snaring birds, which they brought to their whare and preserved in fat in baskets made of bark.

Poor little Hatupatu stayed at home and felt sorry for himself because he was not allowed to go out with them. When they came home to cook their evening meal, they kept the best parts for themselves so that Hatupatu got only the oldest, toughest birds. After a time he became so thin that his ribs could be seen under his skin, but his brothers only laughed at him. Sitting by the fire, red-eyed with the smoke, Hatupatu brooded over his wrongs, and one night he decided that if his brothers would not feed him properly, he would look after himself.

The next day he waited until his brothers had disappeared among the trees and their voices had died away in the distance, and then he hurried to the storehouse. His mouth watered as he looked at the rows and rows of baskets filled with fat, tasty birds. He took some pounded fern-root and sat down to enjoy himself as only a Maori can. He feasted on the tender birds and fern-root till his skin grew tight and he could eat no more. Then he began to think. His brothers would see that someone had been at the stores, for several of the baskets were empty. Hatupatu was afraid. He decided to make it appear that some enemy had raided the storehouse. He knocked over several of the baskets and scattered the contents over the floor. He ran a spear into himself in several places until the blood came, but in such a way that he was not seriously hurt.

When it grew dusk and he heard his brothers returning, he lay down near the whare as though he were unconscious. The brothers found him lying on the path, covered with blood, and believing him to be wounded, they carried him inside and bathed his wounds.

"A war-party came and broke into the storehouse," Hatupatu said in a weak voice. "I tried to keep them off but they attacked me with spears, and then I do not remember anything until I saw you."

They poured melted fat over his wounds and sat down to their evening meal. As usual they took the best and gave a small unappetising share to Hatupatu, but after his morning feast he could not have touched the most tempting morsel, so he went and sat on the smoky side of the fire. His brothers saw his red-rimmed eyes and laughed at him. Hatupatu blinked and coughed in the smoke and smiled secretly to himself.

The following day Hatupatu repeated the performance and the next and the next, until his brothers became suspicious. They left home one morning but returned quietly and looked through the doorway of the storehouse. There was Hatupatu sitting down with a plump bird in his hands, tearing the white flesh with his strong teeth. They watched him get to his feet and begin overturning the baskets, until they could no longer contain their anger. They rushed in and killed him and hid his body under a heap of feathers which had accumulated from all the birds they had plucked.

Soon after this the brothers returned to their home at Rotorua. Their parents greeted them and said, "But where is Hatupatu, your little brother?"

"We do not know. Is he not here?"

"You know very well that he is not here. Where is he?"

They had nothing to say for a moment, and then everybody began to talk at once. "We do not know. We are not supposed to look after him. Perhaps he has run away somewhere. Maybe he is playing a trick and will be here soon."

The father looked at each one in turn until the tongues were stilled, and said shortly, "He is dead. You have killed him."

He went inside his house where he spoke to his wife. "Our sons have killed Hatupatu. He is dead. I can read it in their faces."

"What shall we do?" she asked.

"We will seek him out. I will send a spirit to look for him."

Hatupatu enjoyed the meal unconscious
of the approach of his brothers.

He repeated an incantation and a few moments later a blowfly came blundering inside and buzzed around the room. It was Tamumu – He-that-buzzes-in-the-skies.

"Find my son whose body lies somewhere in the hills before you come to Taupo-moana," Hatupatu's father ordered.

Tamumu flew from the whare, lifting himself above the hills which thrust their broken walls up into the clear air. The myriad facets of his eyes reflected every fold in the ground. After a while Tamumu flew to the ground for he had seen a deserted whare in a clearing. He went to the storehouse and found a huge pile of feathers. Crawling amongst them it was not long before he found the body of Hatupatu. He-who-buzzes-in-the-skies had the ear of the gods, and presently the blood began to course through Hatupatu's veins again, and he stirred. As he rose from his feather resting-place, Tamumu returned to Rotorua.

Hatupatu looked round. His brothers had gone and there was no one there. He snatched up a wooden spear, ran out of the food house and plunged into the forest.

Presently he came upon an old woman who was killing birds. Instead of thrusting a spear gently through the leaves, she crept under the covering of the foliage and speared them with her lips. For a little space Hatupatu stood spellbound, watching her. As she crept quietly up to a tree, he drew back his arm and aimed his spear at a bird. The thin shaft struck a branch and the point flew towards the lips of the woman. She uttered a cry and turned round. Hatupatu ran between the trees, keeping in the shade. Behind him he heard the slow footsteps of the strange woman of the forest, but though he strained every muscle and the sweat dropped from his face, the sound of pursuit grew louder. He stopped under a tree and looked back, his chest heaving, his breath coming in sobbing gasps.

As he watched he saw that there were wings on her arms and she seldom put her feet on the ground. She was coming towards him in long, slow bounds, half flying, half leaping, rising and falling like a bird with clipped wings. In a moment of time she had seen him, and, before he could move, with a little cry she pounced on him. Her bony fingers fastened round his waist and Hatupatu was dragged along a narrow path to a tumble-down whare hidden beneath a clump of nikau palms.

Hatupatu picked up his bundle
and ran into the forest.

"Lie there," she said as she pushed him through the door.

The following morning Hatupatu sat up and looked round him. His captor had brought in a bird. It had not been cooked, but she fell on it and began to tear its flesh with her sharp teeth. When her hunger was satisfied she handed the remains of the bird to the boy. He pretended to eat it, but the raw flesh sickened him, and when the old woman was not looking he slid out of sight.

"Stay here," she said presently, "You cannot escape. If you leave this house I will know that you have gone and I shall catch you and punish you."

When she had left, Hatupatu stood up and examined the whare. A beautiful cloak of red kaka feathers hung on the wall. Beside it there was a cloak of dogskin, and another woven of finest flax. "I should like to take them," Hatupatu thought.

He spoke to the tame birds that fluttered in and out of the door, and the lizards that peered at him with their beady eyes.

"Perhaps she has set them to watch me," he said to himself and shivered as the death omens ran in and out of gaps in the rush walls.

Day after day passed by, and each morning the woman reminded him, "I shall know if you leave." When she said that, Hatupatu felt cold, for her eye was like a lizard's. There was no fire in the whare and he was growing thinner every day for lack of food.

One morning the old woman said, "I am going to a distant part of the country. See that you keep inside the whare. I shall know if you leave!"

As soon as she was out of sight, Hatupatu made a fire and roasted one of the birds. When he had eaten it he lay down to sleep. He was awakened by the sun shining on his face. He looked up at it and said to himself, "She is a long way off now. I may never have such a good chance of escaping again."

He took down the fine cloaks from the wall and made a bundle of them. A taiaha lay in a corner. He picked it up and whirled it round his head, striking down the birds as they fluttered round the house.

"Not one shall escape," he chanted. "I will destroy everything that belongs to the old woman."

He killed the lizards and slashed at the reed frames on the wall. Then he picked up his bundle and ran into the forest. In the whare all the birds and lizards lay still in death – all but one. This bird had hidden in a dark corner and when Hatupatu left it flew through the doorway and straight over the hills to where the old woman was hunting.

Hatupatu ran on swiftly towards his own country with his head over his shoulder. There was no sign of the old woman and he began to feel safe. Presently he lay down to rest. Then he saw the old woman. She was a speck on the distant hills. A few moments later her wings had carried her but a hundred yards from where Hatupatu was resting. The next moment he felt her hot breath on his back. He turned to fly, but his way was barred by a great rock which lay in his path.

"Open, rock!" he called in desperation. The rock swung back and as Hatupatu hurried into the dark it crashed back again. He could hear the old woman beating against it, and the fluttering wings of the little bird. When the sounds had died away, Hatupatu crept out of the rock and hurried on. The sharp eyes of the bird saw him again and Hatupatu hid under the close leaves of a tree until the old woman had gone past. So they went on until they came to Rotorua.

At Whakarewarewa, where the boiling mud stirs and gurgles in the ground, Hatupatu ran lightly between the pools. The woman was almost on top of him. She stretched out her talons to seize him, but the hot steam rose in front of her and blinded her so that she missed her footing and fell into the boiling mud and sank from sight. Hatupatu waved his weapon in triumph and went on until he reached the shores of Lake Rotorua.

Holding his bundle in one hand and the taiaha in the other, he plunged into the waters of the lake and swam across to Mokoia. It was dusk but he could see the warm bathing pool close to his parents' home. He sat down and waited.

When it was quite dark he heard someone coming. The footsteps came closer. Hatupatu could just see a dark shape near the water. He stretched out his hand and seized an ankle. There was a sudden gasp.

"Who are you?" Hatupatu asked in a low voice.

"I am the slave of the old man and the old woman in the whare nearest the pool," was the reply.

"What are you doing here?"

"I have come to get water for them. But who are you?"

"You will see soon enough," Hatupatu said. "Lead me to your whare."

As soon as he entered the dimly lit whare, the old people lifted up their voices. "It is Hatupatu, our son," they cried.

"Be quiet," Hatupatu said in a low voice. "It is indeed Hatupatu. I have risen from the dead. Tamumu brought me back to life, but Tamumu came from my father and mother. I have returned, and I am glad to be here. But you must not weep lest my brothers should hear."

His mother's arms were round him. "We shall protect you now, my son. It is gladness to have our youngest with us. You must not leave us again, Hatupatu."

The boy shook his head. "I know that you will care for me, but my brothers are strong. They must not see me yet. Before daylight comes I will hide in the kumara pit."

"Then I will come and stay with you," his father said.

For several days Hatupatu lay in the kumara pit, but at night he came back to his home again and lay with his father and mother. Time went slowly for Hatupatu because it was dark in the kumara pit, and in the whare there was only a smoky fire. His ears caught all the sounds of the village, and he heard the talking of his brothers. They were grumbling because of the poor food their mother was giving them, little knowing that the best went to Hatupatu.

One morning he heard the sound of voices. He wondered whether someone had seen him and recognised him as he ran from the pit to the whare after dark.

"Hatupatu is here! Hatupatu has come home!" was the cry.

"That is nonsense," he heard his brothers say. "Hatupatu is dead. He cannot come home."

"You said you did not know what had become of him," his father said accusingly.

Before they could reply, Hatupatu rose slowly from the kumara pit. A chief's feathers were in his hair, and down from the breast of an albatross in his ear. His eyes flashed fire.

"Oh, Hatupatu!" his brother jeered when they had recovered from their surprise. "You are pretending to be grown-up, but all the time you have been hiding in the kumara hole like a rat in the ground. You are still a child."

Hatupatu looked at them, only his eyes showing above the ground. "I am older now, my brothers," he said quietly.

"Oh, Hatupatu, you are still a little boasting boy. If you were a man you would come out and fight us."

With a single movement Hatupatu bounded out of the cave, his cloak of red feathers swinging, his taiaha held in his hand.

"This is the weapon I took from Kurangaituku, the bird woman. She lies dead in the mud at Whakarewarewa. This is her cloak." He twitched the cape off his shoulders, flexed his muscles and leaped high in the air.

Hundreds of his brothers' followers had gathered round.

"Ha-nui, Ha-roa, Karika," Hatupatu shouted, addressing himself to his brothers. "I am ready."

The three brothers leapt at him and attempted to take him off guard. Hatupatu stepped backward and turned the strokes of their weapons on his taiaha. They rattled on the stout wood like hail. Then he sprang forward, the taiaha flashing through the air, the tongue darting at the heads of his brothers.

Hatupatu stood back. His brothers were breathing heavily and they came forward warily. Once more the three blades flailed through the air, and once more Hatupatu caught them on his taiaha. It whirled round his head with the sound of a pigeon's wings. In and out went the striking head; crash! The butt came over. The brothers lay still on the ground with the fight all out of them.

"My sons," said the father, "you are very bold when it comes to attacking your younger brother! You would do better to spend your energy in wiping out the insult of Raumati."

The brothers hung their heads. Te Arawa, the canoe, had been burnt by Raumati and the insult had never been wiped out. The tribesmen were waiting for their reply. Ha-nui, the eldest, rose.

I will avenge Te Arawa," he said and went off to his whare.

"I will avenge Te Arawa," said Ha-roa, the second son.

Karika, the third-born, stood up. "I will avenge Te Arawa," he said.

Everyone looked at Hatupatu, but he said nothing and walked into his father's whare.

Hatupatu overcame his three brothers.

A few days later the three brothers manned their canoes and paddled out into the lake. The canoes were loaded with cooked food and the paddle-songs of the leaders floated across the water to where Hatupatu stood with his father. For some days the boy had been learning by heart the tattoo-markings of Raumati,

When the canoes were out of sight, Hatupatu tucked thirty red feather cloaks into his waist band. He did not take any food, but holding his taiaha and other weapons in his hand, he dived into the lake and swam under water. Now and again he came to the surface like a porpoise in the Ocean of Kiwa, to take a breath of air.

Half way across he took a deep breath and dived to the bottom of the lake, coming to the surface with a handful of mussels, which he ate. In this way he stayed his hunger. Soon he could see the canoes ahead of him going through the narrow opening between Rotorua and Rotoiti.

When the canoes came to land, there was Hatupatu standing on the shore with the feather cloaks hung on the trees to dry.

"How did you get here?" his brothers shouted as they sprang ashore. "Where is your canoe?"

"Never mind," said Hatupatu. "I am here. Now I will go with you."

The canoes were left behind and they marched across to Maketu. There they assembled on the beach, a thousand strong. Ha-nui lined them up and divided them between himself and his two brothers, but none were given to Hatupatu.

"Where are my men?" he asked. "I have proved myself a warrior and it is right that I should lead a taua."

They laughed at him. "While you are with us, you are our little brother again," they said. "No one asked you to come. Eating is the only thing you can do. Go and hide behind the toas. This is war, brother, and your stomach, distended with much eating, might be weak."

Hatupatu had expected that his brothers would refuse his request, so without further argument he went away by himself, taking his thirty cloaks with him. After a little search he found a glade where he could sleep undisturbed. He woke up early the next morning and even in the half light he saw at once that the place he had chosen was ideal for his purpose. Dotted about the slopes were clumps of fern and tussock and creeping plants. Working quickly, he tied the bushes with flax and dressed them with the feather cloaks until at a little distance they looked like a band of warriors crouching for the attack.

The sun was now creeping over the hills. Hatupatu looked around him. Far away he could see the converging lines as the enemy tribes gathered together from their pas. A scout had brought them word of the invasion of their tribal grounds, and the chiefs were advancing to the attack.

Closer at hand his brothers were marching up and down in front of their men. Their voices came to him clearly in the still air. When they had finished, Hatupatu sprang to his feet and began to encourage his tussock and bushes. His brothers' warriors turned to look at him. His long hair was tied in four knots, in each of which was a bunch of feathers. A murmur of admiration ran through their ranks, for Hatupatu was a toas's toa – tall and straight with a quickness on his feet and a length of reach which would stand him in good stead in any fight.

When he had finished, Hatupatu ran behind the bushes and unloosened three of his head-knots, leaving one over his forehead. He threw a red feather cloak round him and, stepping out again, he addressed his mock troops.

To the warriors by the shore, it appeared as though another chief was exhorting the little band. He sat down, and presently stood up in another place wearing a flax cloak with his hair hanging loose. Many times did Hatupatu sit down, and many times he rose. Each time he was dressed differently. His cloaks were of dogskin, feather and flax, and in his hand he waved mere and patupatu and taiaha. At length he stood up naked, ready for the fight, with his white bone patu quivering in his hand.

"Aah!" breathed his brothers' warriors, and "Aah!" said the men of Raumati who had drawn close. They were brave men, eager for the fray, but they avoided the tiny band of warriors with the many powerful chiefs.

They ran swiftly towards Ha-nui's men, and as they drew near they threw their light manuka spears until the air seemed full of flying weapons. Raumati's men pressed home their advantage. Ha-nui's line of warriors wavered and broke and the men of Raumati were amongst them like a breaking wave on the sand. Ha-roa's men were close behind and the defence stiffened. A double row of warriors awaited the assault, but again Raumati and his men swept through them and on to the third line which was led by Karika. Here the brothers of Hatupatu made their last stand. The line held. Karika plunged into the thickest of the fight and his men began to edge forward so that Raumati's warriors felt the pressure against them. They began to give way. Then Raumati's voice was heard calling on them for further effort. They were seasoned warriors and the response was instant. Once more they surged forward, right through Karika's toas who broke and fled for their lives towards the shelter of the forest.

As they pursued the retreating forces of Mokoia, Raumati and his men heard a loud voice chanting a war song. They turned round and saw, far away, the small taua near the bush with its leader standing in front waving his mere.

"Turn on them again; turn on them again," came the strong voice of Hatupatu.

Raumati called his men who made their way cautiously towards the forces of the many rangatiras. For a while they were lost to sight, for the ground rose and fell. Before they reached the crest of the last rise the bushes were brushed aside and Hatupatu stood in front of them. He had flung off his cloak, his hair was unadorned, and in his right hand he held his mere. A chief sprang forward from the advancing taua and struck a blow which would have ended the fight at once had his weapon reached its mark, but Hatupatu deflected it with his mere. He closed on the chief and in the time that is taken in drawing a deep breath, Raumati's man lay lifeless on the ground.

Panic seized the warriors, for the chief had been a fighter of renown. They turned round and fled down the slope. Hatupatu filled his lungs and his song of triumph rose above the clamour of the retreating toas. Lurking in the distant forest his brothers heard that jubilant cry. Peering through the undergrowth they saw Raumati's warriors streaming towards them. They called their men together hastily and fell upon the rout, while Hatupatu ran to and fro seeking a chief who bore the tattoo marks that he had learned from his father.

Each brother claimed that he had
captured the head of Raumati.

In Mokoia the old men, women and children crowded to the water's edge to see the returning warriors. The chant of victory swelled across the lake as the rowers sent the canoes surging over the water to run halfway up the shelving beach.

The old man, the father of Hatupatu, stood erect on the beach facing his sons.

"You have conquered, my children," he said as the song ended.

"We have conquered," Ha-nui replied. "The enemy has perished. This is the great deed of your sons, of Ha-nui, of Ha-roa, of Karika, that will be sung by our children in days to come."

Ha-nui stood up on the canoe, "Raumati has fallen to my hand," he said, holding up the head of a warrior.

But see, Ha-roa is holding up another head, and Karika yet a third.

"This is Raumati!" Ha-nui said fiercely. "He led his people. With my own hand I killed him."

"No, this is Raumati," shouted Ha-roa.

"You, my father, will judge. From Karika has come the vengeance that was spent on Raumati," said the third son.

Their father turned from one to another and then bent his head and looked at the ground. "Aue!" he said. "Aue! You could not tell. Raumati has escaped."

Then Hatupatu stood up. He had been seated in the midst of the warriors where he could not be seen. He brought his hand from under his cloak and held up a tattooed head.

"Truly you shall be the judge, my father," he said softly, but everyone heard his voice in the silence that had fallen. "Is this the head of your enemy!"

Hi father lifted his eyes and light came back to them. "Yes," he said, "Yes, that is Raumati. Now is our triumph. It is Hatupatu, my youngest, who has avenged the insult to our people. It is Hatupatu who will be honoured!"

The firelight danced on the people as they gave themselves up to rejoicing that night, and of all who were there, Hatupatu, bravest and strongest, was the honoured chief. But in the darkness of their lonely whares the songs and laughter were bitterness to Ha-nui, Ha-roa, and Karika.

14

Whakatau-Potiki

Whakatau-Potiki looked with pride across the harbour, for there were no less than a thousand canoes floating on the still water. A large war party had gathered to avenge the death of his brother Tu-whakararo at the hands of the treacherous Ati-Hapai. Quantities of fern-root had been prepared as food, and the women of the tribe sang songs to inflame the warriors before they went out to battle.

Whakatau made his preparations carefully. All day the canoes sailed on until they came to the mouth of a river. The taua landed and the warriors were told that the stream had to be crossed. Some of them tried to jump over but failed, and others said that it was hopeless to wade across such a swift-running stream. Whakatau led a body of picked men up to the bank. They made a tremendous leap which carried them to the far side of the stream.

The leader realised that numbers do not always count. Perhaps it would be better if he were to take a few chosen warriors who would be able to do anything he required of them, rather than a huge army of untrained men.

As night fell he picked out his chosen men and gave them their orders. They crept quietly from canoe to canoe, pulling out the plugs of every one except the leader's.

The next morning the order to embark was given, and the fleet put out from the shore. In a little while it was seen that the canoes were beginning to fill with water. The paddlers turned hastily and went back to the beach, leaving only Whakatau's canoe afloat. The crew took no notice of the abandoned warriors, but paddled on until they came to the Ati-Hapai village. Whakatau had painted his canoe white on one side and black on the other. Presently the Ati-Hapa people came down to the shore. Someone pointed to Whakatau's canoe, which lay at a distance, and asked whether it was a canoe or a seal. Some of the men swam out to see for themselves. The most powerful swimmer forged ahead until he came close enough to see that it was indeed a canoe that lay on the water. He raised himself out of the water and called to the steersman, "Turn back! Turn back!"

Then he dived and swam under water until he came to the bow of the canoe, intending to come up suddenly and take Whakatau by surprise; but while he was still under the surface Whakatau killed him with his spear. One after the other the swimmers came close, and each was killed by Whakatau and his warriors. Mongotipi was the only one who escaped. He swam ashore and told his people that a great warrior was in the canoe, and that they must be careful.

Among the Ati-Hapai there were two men of great renown. One had the power of flying through the air, and the other of walking on the water. As soon as he heard what the swimmer had to say, the flying man sprang up into the air and flew towards the canoe. Whakatau saw him coming and hastily built a perch, such as birds alight upon. When the flying man saw the perch, he dropped down and stood on it, brandishing his weapon. But, like the perch that is set by a stream in the forest, the perch on the great waka of Whakatau was also furnished with a snare. The flying man was caught by the feet, and he too joined the swimmers who had been sent so quickly to the Rarohenga (the underworld of departed spirits) by Whakatau and his men.

When he saw what had happened to his friend who flew through the air, the walker-on-water came swiftly towards the canoe. Whakatau filled a calabash with appetising fat and set it floating on the waves. Presently the walker smelled the pleasant odour. He went up to the calabash and gulped down the fat; but alas, Whakatau had concealed a fish hook in it, and the helpless water-walker was pulled up to the canoe and killed.

That night Whakatau and his men crept ashore quietly. Whakatau was disguised as a slave. He went inside Te Uru-o-manono, the famous circular house of the Ati-Hapai tribe. No one took any notice of the unknown slave, who listened to the people talking excitedly over the day's events. They wondered where the strange canoe had come from and who was the mighty rangatira in command of it.

As they talked, there came a rattling of bones from the ceiling

The flying man was caught by the snare on the perch
that Whakatau had tied to the canoe.

of the house. The bones of Tu-whakararo were calling out for vengeance.

Someone asked Mongotipi, who had seen the captain of the strange canoe before he escaped, what he was like.

"He is such a great one that I cannot describe him," Mongotipi replied. "He is a rangatira of rangatiras."

"Is he like me?" different ones asked him. No, he was not like any of the Ati-Hapai people.

Whakatau straightened himself and sprang to his feet.

"Is he like me?" he demanded.

They all stared at him, but Mongotipi drew back aghast. "That is the man!" he exclaimed.

For a moment there was silence, and then everyone rushed towards Whakatau. He snatched up a calabash of water and emptied it over the fire, so that the whare was plunged into darkness. Men fell over each other and caught hold of their fellows. There was shouting and confusion everywhere, while men rushed to and fro in the dark. Whakatau climbed up to the roof and took down the bones of his brother. Then he slid cautiously out of the house and barricaded the door.

Outside the great house Te Uru-o-manono were the invading warriors and their leader Whakatau-potiki. Inside were their enemies, the Ati-Hapai. Someone handed a torch to Whakatau, and he held it to the thatch, which burst into flame with a rush and a roar that drowned the cries of his enemies.

Far over the sea the mother of Whakatau-potiki and Tu-whakararo sat staring at the horizon, because she knew that there stood the house of Te Uru-o-manono. All was dark. There was no moon, and only the bright stars speckled the black sky..

Suddenly a red glare shot across the water, and as the dark sky reflected the leaping flames, the sorrowing mother knew that the death of her son had been avenged.

15

Hinemoa and Tutanekai

In the midst of tales of battle and sudden death, of gigantic feasting and fabulous monsters, of the unearthly patupaiarehe, the strange fairies of the forest, comes the simple love-tale of Hinemoa and Tutanekai.

On the island of Mokoia, set like a jewel on the shining surface of Rotorua, Tutanekai lived with his mother and stepfather and his half-brothers. Cut off from the people of the mainland, they lived their placid island life untroubled by the tribal wars that raged among the people of the lake-shore. But they were not entirely isolated. Now and again the canoes that visited the mainland brought back news of the outer world. It was in such a way as this that Tutanekai and his brothers came to hear of Hinemoa, the beautiful high-born girl of Owhata. All who spoke of her told of her gentleness and beauty and strength of character. These reports so stirred the brothers that they fell in love with her before ever they saw her. The brothers of Tutanekai each boasted that he would take her to wife, but Tutanekai himself said nothing. He went out on the balcony of his hillside whare at night and looked across the dark water towards Owhata. Then he would sigh, and after a while he would bring out his flute and breathe a love-song into it.

The music carried clearly across the water and Hinemoa, sitting in the moonlight with her friends, would fall silent. The steam by the lakeside drifted above the manuka, restless and lost, like the thoughts of Hinemoa. She had heard of the brothers of Mokoia, and she would smile to herself and say, "That is the music of Tutanekai."

One day there was a great meeting of the tribes on the mainland. Hinemoa was there with her people, and her eyes sought out Tutanekai. Some instinct seemed to tell her that the tall, handsome young man was the flute-player of the moonlight nights. As for Tutanekai, he had seen many young girls, but of all the lovely young women of Rotorua who were gathered in the house of meeting, it was only Hinemoa who attracted him. In this way they became lovers, yet neither Hinemoa nor Tutanekai declared their love. The young woman of Owhata was a high-born, of the line of the chiefs, a puhi, and although he loved her, Tutanekai feared to risk a refusal. Yet at every gathering he sought her and spoke to her in friendly fashion. Finally he decided to send a message to her. It was taken by a friend. When this friend had told of Tutanekai's love, Hinemoa said simply, "E-hu! Have we then each loved alike?"

The next time the tribes gathered together, the lovers met outside the meeting-house. No one missed them, for the whare was full. While the laughter and cries of the dancers were loud in their ears, they sat outside in the darkness, and Tutanekai told Hinemoa his words of love. "How shall we meet?" he asked. Hinemoa's voice replied softly, "I will come to you, Tutanekai, my beloved. I must go when no one suspects, and you must be ready for me. How shall I know when you will be waiting?"

Tutanekai thought for a moment. "Already the music has carried my love to you across the waters of Rotorua. Now let it bear another message – the message that I am waiting for you. When you hear the music in the silence of the night, you will know that I am looking for your canoe to steal across the shadowed lake."

The next night Hinemoa heard the distant flute, and stole down to the shore of the lake where the canoes were kept. They were all there, but alas, someone had beached them, and they were high up on the land. Not a single canoe was floating in the water. She could hear the music clearly across the water where the island of Mokoia lay sleeping on the quiet lake.

"Hinemoa! Hinemoa!" called the flute. "Hinemoa!" and her heart was heavy in her because of her longing for her lover. She turned away. Her people must have seen the manner of Tutanekai's glance in the meeting-house. Perhaps someone had heard them whispering together in the darkness, for it was unusual for all the canoes to be beached at the same time.

The following night she went to the lakeside, but still the canoes were high and dry, and her suspicion turned to certainty.

Every night Tutanekai's music called to her. The moon waxed and waned while love for him stirred in her so that she could not sleep, and the distant flute seemed to thunder in her ears. With her eyes closely shut, she could see Tutanekai on the balcony of his house blowing into the long putorino and then putting it down and straining his eyes to see if he could catch sight of the darker shape of a canoe amongst the shadows.

Then came the moonless nights and she could wait no longer. The rows of canoes had mocked her every night and she did not even glance towards them. She had prepared six large dried gourds, tying them together with flax so that they would support her in the water.

As she went towards the little beach, Tutanekai's music sounded again and she quickened her resolve. She threw off her single garment, a cloak of finely woven flax, tied the gourds under her armpits and waded out until she found herself being lifted by the waves. She struck out boldly. She felt like a bird which has escaped from a cage.

Presently the lapping of the waves seemed to drown the sound of the flute. Perhaps a current of air had carried the sound away from her, but she felt a moment of panic. The darkness pressed down on her like a solid wall. She tried to lift herself up to see if the island was close at hand but the darkness closed in on her. She had lost her sense of direction. She could not tell where Mokoia lay, nor the beach she had left. Her arms were tired and the gourds seemed to have lost their buoyancy, so that the little waves struck cruelly against her face, and the water was cold.

She gave a cry of despair as something brushed against her face. Then with a sob of relief she caught hold of it and rested against it. It was a tree trunk floating in the water. As she held closely to it and raised herself a little above the waves, the wind brought the sound of the flute back to her ears. She pushed away from the log and began to swim steadily towards the music.

The gloom had lightened and she could even see the bulk of the island against the faint starlight. Sometimes she grew tired and rested, but her panic was over. Once the current carried her away from the island, but she swam more strongly and felt the water surging under her. The time passed slowly and the water grew colder. Then the music stopped and the only sound was the ceaseless lapping of the waves against her breast. She stopped and

Hinemoa felt the ground under her feet.

listened. At first she could hear nothing. Then a tiny sound – a crash and a hiss like a wave falling on the sand and running up the slope of the beach. Another hiss as it drained away, carrying a myriad grains of sand with it. A moment later she felt the ground under her feet.

She stumbled up the beach, half frozen. The cold wind numbed her flesh even more than the lake water. Feeling her way with her hands in front of her, she came upon some rocks. They were warm, and she could smell the sulphur-laden steam of a hot pool. Once before she had been on the island, and she knew where she was. This was the hot pool of Waikimihia, directly below Tutanekai's whare.

She lowered herself gratefully into the water and felt warmth soaking into her chilled body.

Now that she had reached her lover's home and the dangers of the journey were behind her, she suddenly felt shy and reluctant to appear before him. Her clothes lay far away on the beach at Owhata. Then came the sound of footsteps descending the path toward Waikimihia. In a flash she pulled herself towards the bank and crouched under an overhanging rock.

The footsteps stopped, something dropped into the pool, and she heard the water gurgling into a calabash close by her side. Disguising her voice, she said in a deep voice, "Where are you taking the water? Who are you?"

The man who was fetching the water started at the voice coming from the darkness.

"I am the slave of Tutanekai. I am taking the water to him."

Hinemoa's heart leaped. "Give me the calabash," she said, still pretending to be a man. She spoke so confidently that the slave handed the calabash to her without protest. She put it to her lips and drank. Then, rising her arm, she hurled the empty vessel across the pool so that it smashed against the rocks on the further side.

The slave cried out, half in fear and half in anger, "Why have you done that? That was Tutanekai's calabash."

Hinemoa made no reply, but only drew back further into the shadow of the rock. The slave looked carefully over the stones but could see nothing. "Who are you?" he called shrilly, and when there was no reply, he turned and ran up to the whare.

"What is the matter?" Tutanekai exclaimed as he saw the slave's face. "What has happened? Where is the water I told you to bring?"

"The calabash is broken."

"Who broke it?"

"The man in the pool."

Tutanekai looked at him closely. "Can you not speak more clearly? Who broke it?"

"The man in the pool," the slave repeated doggedly.

For a moment Tutanekai thought of going down to find out for himself, but he changed his mind. Night after night he had played his flute, but Hinemoa had forgotten. He turned his face to the wall and said wearily, "Oh, take another calabash and fetch the water."

The slave departed on his errand a second time. He looked around cautiously but there was no sign of any stranger, yet no sooner had he dipped the calabash in the pool than the deep voice called out, "If that water is for Tutanekai, give it to me."

The slave's legs trembled, but he held out the calabash at arm's length. A hand came out of the shadows, and again the calabash crashed against the rocks and broke.

This time the man did not wait to protest. He ran up the winding path as swiftly as his legs would carry him.

"The second calabash had been broken by the man at the pool," he gasped.

Tutanekai shut his eyes. "Take another calabash," he said in a flat voice.

In a little while the slave stood before him empty-handed once more. At last Tutanekai felt the anger rising swiftly in him. He forgot his longing for Hinemoa. With one swift movement he sprang to his feet, caught up his mere and ran down to the pool.

Hinemoa heard him coming and knew it was her lover. The slave's footsteps had been heavy and slow; Tutanekai was running lightly and swiftly. She crouched still further under the rocks and held her breath as the footsteps stopped on the brink of the pool. The moon was rising and she saw his shadow lying across the water. Under the rocks the darkness lay heavily.

"Where are you, breaker of pots?" called Tutanekai. "Come out so that I can see you. Show yourself like a man instead of hiding like a koura, a crayfish, in the water."

There was no reply. Peering through her hair, Hinemoa saw the shadow moving across the water, coming closer and closer.

A hand reached down and touched her hair. "Ah!" cried Tutanekai, "I have found you. Come out, you rascal." His grip tightened. "Let me see your face."

Hinemoa stood up. Climbing slowly on to the bank, she faced her lover, beautiful and shy like the silver heron which is seen but once in a hundred years. "I am Hinemoa," she whispered.

The harshness fled from Tutanekai's face like summer clouds before the sun.

"Hinemoa!"

The smoke from the cooking fires rose straight up in the morning air as the people ate their breakfast.

"Where is Tutanekai?" someone asked.

There was no reply until his slave stepped forward. "I have not seen him since he went down to the stranger at the pool in the night," he said.

"What stranger?" they asked, and he told them of the breaking of the calabashes, and how Tutanekai went down himself to meet the stranger.

"This is strange to my ears," one of the old men said. "Perhaps something has happened to Tutanekai? He is a bold fighter, but in the night even the bravest may be worsted when the shadows conceal the thrust of a hidden weapon. Hurry to his whare and see if all is well with him."

Their eyes followed the slave as he hastened to the home of Tutanekai. In the stillness the sound of the sliding door striking the frame came like a thunder-clap.

He peered into the gloom and then went back to the people waiting on the marae. "There are four feet there," he cried. "I looked for Tutanekai and I saw four feet instead of two."

A murmur of voices came from the men and women. "Who is with him?" the old man called, raising his voice so that he could be heard.

The slave did not answer but ran back again to look. He returned, shouting with excitement, "It is Hinemoa!"

His cry was taken up by the people. "Hinemoa is here with Tutanekai!"

Now Tutanekai's brothers were jealous, for they had each thought that Hinemoa would choose him for her husband. "It cannot be Hinemoa," they shouted angrily. "There is no canoe on the beach, so she could not have come during the night. The slave is lying."

Then Tutanekai came out of the whare, leading Hinemoa by the hand. She held herself proudly, wearing a cloak of her husband's, and walking by his side. A great cry of welcome went up from the people, drowning the brothers' angry exclamations. "It is indeed Hinemoa. Welcome to Hinemoa!"

That is the love story of Hinemoa and her daring journey across the lake to her lover, which will be told so long as the Arawa people live by the steaming waters of Rotorua.

16

Tura and Whiro

The great chief Whiro* had committed an evil deed which brought on him the displeasure of his people. He was unhappy and, finding no pleasure in life, he determined to destroy himself. He made friends with another chief named Tura, and proposed that they should make a long canoe voyage together. Tura had no idea of Whiro's real purpose, and was enthusiastic about the idea.

He left his wife and baby son and the two friends set out on their journey and soon lost sight of land. Far out at sea they saw a black speck on the horizon. As they drew closer they found to their surprise that it was another canoe. Tu-tatahau, the captain of the canoe, hailed them saying, "Canoe! Whose canoe are you?"

One of Whiro's men answered insolently, "Can you not see? This is a canoe of the gods."

Tu-tatahau was exasperated and threw his spear, killing the speaker.

"Who are you?" he repeated. "Is it a crew of men?"

Another paddler replied, "You have been told. It is a canoe of the gods."

Tu-tatahau threw a second spear, and though the paddler saw it coming and leaned to one side, he was not quick enough. The heavy weapon pinned his body to the side of the canoe.

Once again came the query, "Whose canoe are you?"

Whiro whispered to Tura, "This is a powerful chief and one to be feared. What shall we do?"

"Leave it to me," answered Tura. Standing up and raising his voice he cried, "This is the canoe of Whiro. It is the canoe of the ancient ones who rend and tear."

---

* This is Whiro the explorer, and is not to be confused with Whiro the tipua and god of evil.

Tu-tatahau trembled when he heard these words. He gave an order to his men, who thrust their paddles into the waves. The water boiled under them as the canoe turned and sped away.

Presently Whiro and Tura came in sight of the coast of a new country and turned towards it. They did not land but sailed close to the coast. A strong current and a steady breeze carried the canoe so swiftly along the shore that Tura, who had learned something of Whiro's character in the brief time he had been with him, was frightened, believing that the canoe was headed for disaster. They were so close to the shore that they were sometimes swept under the branches of trees. Tura made a sudden leap and clutched at a bough, swinging himself to land before anyone could prevent him. The canoe rushed onwards and was quickly lost to sight.

Tura heaved a sigh of relief, but he was lonely and perplexed. He thought that if he went inland he might meet people who would give him food and shelter. He walked on for the rest of the day, but met no one, and at night he lay down to sleep, tired, hungry and thirsty. By the end of the following day he was even more weary, but at nightfall he came to a decrepit whare. The only occupant was an old woman who fed him with fruit and water and gave him a mat to lie on. He stayed there for several days, and in his loneliness and anxiety for companionship he offered to marry her.

"No," said the woman. "I am old and useless, and I have been placed here to guard this place. There are plenty of young women who would be glad to have you."

She took him to the kainga, where Tura was amazed to find that everyone lived in trees. They were peculiar people called the Aitanga-a-nuku-mai-tore. They had large bodies and small heads. Tura chose one of them for his wife, and as he could not speak her language very well, he called her Turaki-hau, and said that his name was Wai-rangi. His wife put food in front of him, but when he went to eat it he drew back in disgust, for there was only raw meat, and green grass, and uncooked roots.

"These people cannot be men and women," he said to himself fearfully. "They must be gods or Turehu. I must be careful."

Fortunately he had brought with him his fire-making tools. He got his wife to put her foot on the flat board and rubbed the pointed stick rapidly backwards and forwards along the groove. As the smoke curled up she began to shake with fear; and as the smoking tinder burst into flame she hid behind a tree. When Tura looked up he saw that the strange people had all disappeared. He made an oven, lit a fire under the stones, and caught hold of his wife's cloak. When he saw that she would not run away in spite of her fear, he cooked the food she had already prepared. As they ate it together, the savoury smell was wafted through the trees, and the Aitanga came creeping back through the trees to see for themselves what wonderful things Wai-rangi was doing. He offered some of the cooked food to them and they tasted it, cautiously at first, but with growing enthusiasm when they realised how good it was.

Gradually Tura became used to their ways and learnt more about them. The time came when Turaki-hau was to give birth to a child. He built a special house for her, and her relatives brought gifts – soft, scaped flax and sharp, knife-like flakes of obsidian.

Tura was surprised that the presents would be given before the baby was born, and asked why they came so soon. His wife looked at him and he was surprised to see the tears rolling down her cheeks.

"Why are you crying" he asked.

"It is because the time has come to leave you, Wai-rangi."

"Why should you leave me? Are you not happy with me?"

"You know that you have brought happiness into my life, but my baby will soon be born, and then I must die."

Tura was taken aback. "But when your baby is born it will need you to take care of it."

She was equally surprised. "Surely you know that mothers must lose their lives when their babies are born?"

Tura smiled. "I do not! Your people have strange customs. Now I see that I must teach you the customs of my people. Trust me, and do not be afraid."

He went outside and sent the women back to their homes in the trees. He built another house, and in it he erected two strong poles. One he called Pou-tama-tane and the other Pou-tama-wahine.

"This is the post for boys," he said. "Lean your back against it. The other is the post for girls. Hold on to it and all will be well. If the baby is not born soon, say these words," and he taught her the chant used by the women of his country.

"If the baby is still not born say, "One for Tura!" and you will find that you and your baby will both be well."

Then for the first time Turaki-hau knew her husband's name. It gave her strength, and presently a baby boy was born; and to the amazement of her relatives, Turaki was able to hold him in her arms and sing a lullaby to him.

A year passed by, and the baby had grown into a little boy who could walk without help. One day Tura was lying on his back while his wife combed his hair. She gave an exclamation of surprise.

"What is the matter?" he asked.

"Look! There are some white hairs among the black ones!"

Tura laughed. "They are the signs of age and decay, but I have a long time to live yet."

She looked at him seriously. "Do you mean that men of your world must grow old and die?"

"Yes. It will happen to all of us some day."

"No, Tura. Death is not known in my world except when mothers die for their children."

She got up and ran into the house. Tura was thoughtful as he sat under the trees. He realised for the first time that his wife really belonged to the Aitanga and was not a mortal like himself. He picked up the child and wept over him, wondering whether he would grow into a man like his father, or whether he would be like his mother's people.

He knew that he could no longer stay with them but must try to go back to the men and women of his own world. He wept over the boy for two days, and for two days Turaki-hau wept over her husband.

He packed the few things he had brought with him, pressed noses with his little son and said, "Farewell. Live a good and quiet life, my son, and do no evil."

He walked through the forest for three days until he came to the shore. He stared over the water hoping that he might see a canoe belonging to his own people, but the sea was empty. He had come so far from his homeland with Whiro that there was little chance of seeing a canoe. He sighed and wept a little for he could not live with an alien people, and he had no companions.

He built two whatas, or food stores, on strong posts. One was

Tura took leave of his family.

tall and the other, which he intended to keep for his old age when he would no longer be able to climb a ladder, was built near the ground. Finally he made a house and went out to get food. He did not have to look far, for close at hand a whale had been stranded on the beach. He cut it up and dried the flesh. Some he put on the high stage and the rest in the low whata.

The days and years went by. The grey hairs multiplied until no black ones were left. Tura grew old and bent and moved about with difficulty. The weakness of extreme age overcame him and he could not care for himself. He grew thin and emaciated and dirty, and his hair was long and tangled. His thoughts went back to the time when he was young and lived happily with his first wife in his own country. He remembered his son, his first son born to him by a human mother.

"O Ira-tu-roto! Ira-tu-roto!" he cried, thinking of the boy still as a baby, when he had seen him last.

Ira-tu-roto, living far across the sea, was now a grown man with children of his own. That night he had a vivid dream. When he woke he said to his wife and children, "I dreamt that I saw my father Tura, who was lost long ago when he went on a voyage with Whiro. He was old and helpless in my dream, and he kept called, "O Ira-tu-roto! Ira-tu-roto!"

His wife said, "It was only a dream. Your father has been dead for many years."

That night the dream came back to him, stronger than ever. He rose from his wife's side and went to his mother.

"It is my father," he said simply. "He needs me."

The old woman nodded. "You must do what you must, my son."

Ira said, "Give me some of your sweet-scented oil."

He anointed himself from head to foot and took the oil with him. Quietly he roused his slaves and some of his companions. They crept out of the house. Ira-tu-roto's mother was the only woman who was awake. She said nothing but followed them with her eyes, sitting motionless on her mat.

They ran the canoe down the shingle beach in the starlight and launched it in the moving waters. The paddles bit deep and the canoe headed eastwards and was out of sight when the sun rose. Every night Ira-tu-roto heard his father's voice, coming closer but seeming to grow weaker.

They came to a place where the current ran swiftly past the shore, and as the canoe was swept along they saw a tiny whare and two whatas, one tall, the other short.

The paddles dipped deep again and the canoe was forced against the current into a sheltered bay.

Ira-tu-roto was the first to enter the tiny house. When his eyes became accustomed to the gloom he saw an old man lying on a tattered mat. His bones showed through the withered skin, his flowing locks fell over his shoulders and breast, and he muttered in his sleep. His body was dirty and neglected.

The visitor bent over and put his ear close to the old man's mouth and for the last time he heard the whispered words, "O Ira-tu-roto! Ira-tu-roto!"

Lifting him up tenderly, he called to his slaves who brought food and water. Dried kumara was crumbled in the water and fed to Tura. Ira washed him and anointed him with the remainder of his mother's oil. The old man was too frail to be seated in the canoe. They built a box, lined it with moss, set it in the canoe and laid him in it.

Tura could see the blue sky and the wind-chased clouds by day and the wheeling stars at night. He heard the splash of water on the sides of the canoe. He felt the rhythm of strong arms and paddles and the song of the leader – of Ira-tu-roto, his son. He was going home!

17

The Fairy People

Ruarangi and the Turehu

Many stories are told of the fair-skinned fairy people who live in the forests of Aotearoa. The Maori called them Turehu or Patupaiarehe. They were a weird race, not human, yet with the shape of human beings. They loved the dense bush country and were at home in the hills, where they lived in the remote fastnesses of the forest.

On the slopes of Pirongia, the sentinel of the Waikato, lived Ruarangi and his wife. While the husband was absent on a journey, one of the Turehu crept from the forest and carried off his wife.

Poor Ruarangi was distracted when he returned home and found that his wife was gone. He knew that she had not run away, as some of his friends suggested, because they were very happy in their married life. Taking his spear and his greenstone club with him, Ruarangi searched far and wide. He even went up the steep gullies of Pirongia where the trees met together overhead and long festoons of creepers trailed from the gnarled, moss-covered trunks and the half-light of the evening was caught in a mesh of green leaves. This was fairy country indeed, but Ruarangi's eyes glowed fiercely and there was no fear in his heart, only hate for the fair-skinned half-men who he believed had stolen his wife.

As he lay back on the damp moss after eating his food one day, just as twilight dimmed the bush, he rubbed his eyes and sprang up with a shout. On the other side of the creek he saw his wife, and with her one of the dreaded Turehu.

To his amazement, his wife looked at him and then turned away and began to run between the trees. For a moment Ruarangi could hardly believe his eyes; then he knew that she must be bewitched. Pausing only to snatch up his weapons, he ran after the escaping pair.

The Turehu man ran noiselessly, but Ruarangi could hear his

wife as she broke through the twigs and branches. Soon he knew he was overtaking her, for the sounds grew louder. He came to a place where the trees had fallen and grass carpeted the level ground. The Turehu was urging his wife across to the shelter of the trees.

Ruarangi stopped and took careful aim. His slender spear sang through the air, straight for the half-man; but some power seemed to turn it aside and it slid past and stuck quivering in the ground.

In a moment the fugitives would be gone. The light was growing very dim, and Ruarangi was afraid he would lose them in the darkness. He still had the remains of his cooked dinner with him, and his hand closed over a steamed kumara. His wife and the Turehu were now right on the edge of the forest, but the missile went true to its mark and struck his wife on the back.

Ruarangi's heart leaped, for he realised that cooked food would break the spell that had been cast by the fairy. For a moment his wife stood still, then she pulled her hand away from her captor and turned round. There was her husband, standing waiting for her! With a cry of joy she rang to him and threw herself into his arms.

Husband and wife made all the haste they could through the trackless bush, bumping into trees and tripping over roots, anxious to get away from the fearful home of the Turehu. At last they came out of the forest and saw the lower slopes of Pirongia lying quiet and unafraid in the silver moonlight.

At first Ruarangi would not listen to his wife as they lay in the whare, but soothed her with comforting words. She could not remember much about her life with the Turehu. She shivered when she heard the dreaded name, and Ruarangi would not speak about them. The next morning she seemed more like her old self and said, "We must be very careful. The Turehu man will come back for me."

"How can we prevent him?" asked Ruarangi. "Is there anything the Turehu are afraid of?"

His wife thought for a moment. "Yes," she said, "kokowai! Red ochre! They are afraid of the sacred colour."

Several days went by and there was no sign of the fair-skinned people of the forest. Ruarangi's wife was beginning to lose her fear. But one evening, as they stood before the whare, she gave a shriek. "Look!" she cried. The Turehu half-man was coming towards them with great strides.

The Turehu leapt frantically from
place to place to avoid the red ochre.

Husband and wife both ran inside their whare. Ruarangi snatched up the red ochre and smeared some on his wife. At that moment the half-man sprang inside the door. He seemed enormous in the dim light. His teeth were bared and his white skin glowed with a cold radiance. Coldness seemed to come into the whare with him.

Ruarangi smeared the kokowai over himself and shouted, "You cannot touch us."

The half-man shrank back as he saw the sacred colour. Ruarangi brushed it against the door. With a low moan the fairy visitor sprang through the window. The infuriated husband followed. He smeared the kokowai on the ground while the Turehu man sprang from one place to another. Presently there were few places left on the marae for him to stand. When he saw that everything was protected by the sacred colour which he dared not touch, he jumped to the roof of Ruarangi's whare in a single bound, looked round the kainga sorrowfully and began to sing a song of farewell, for he too had loved Ruarangi's woman. The people of the village crept fearfully from their homes at the sound of that ghostly voice. There were tears in it, and they never forgot it, the song of farewell from Turehu to Maori. Then he leaped to the ground and was gone, like a ghostly moth in the moonlight.

Ah, it is true, they say. And if you mark your door with red ochre, you will never be troubled with Turehu or Patupaiarehe in your home.

How Men Learned the Art of Carving

The boys of the kainga came up to Rua-pupuke, the water running from them and falling on the ground.

"Your son!" they panted.

Rua-pupuke raised his head sharply. "My son? What have you to say about my son?"

"We were swimming," one of the boys said, "when suddenly he disappeared. He did not cry out and the sea was calm. We were playing in the water, and when we looked he had gone."

Rua sprang to his feet and ran down to the beach and along the reef that stretched out into the deep water, casting his cloak from his shoulders as he ran.

"Where did you last see him?" he asked.

The pointed to the place. Rua slid silently into the water and disappeared from view. The boys waited for him to come up, but nothing broke the surface and the eddies died away.

Down and down went Rua, swimming into the dim underworld of the water like a fish. He was a powerful chief and a tohunga. Even as he ran he had been preparing himself for his quest by calling on his spirit, for he knew that his son had been captured by the Ponaturi, the water fairies or goblins who live on the seabed.

Presently the shape of a house seemed to swim waveringly towards him. It was not like the plain houses of the men of that far-away time. Every board was carved into wonderful designs, and for eyes the figures had shining silver paua shell cunningly set in them. On the gable of the house was a life-like figure set as a tekoteko. It was his son.

Rua took no notice of him but entered the richly ornamented doorway. There was no one inside except an old woman whose eyes lit up when she saw him.

"I knew you would come. You are Rua-pupuke," she said.

Where are the Ponaturi?" asked Rua.

"They are away at their work. If you help me to block up the holes in the walls, we can hold them until the light comes and they will die."

Without a word Rua helped to block up all the chinks in the boards. At nightfall the Ponaturi rushed into the house with a noise like that of a thundering waterfall.

During the night Rua lifted his son from his place on the gable and swam with him to the surface and took him to the kainga. Then he returned to the home of the Ponaturi.

When the sun was high and the water had turned to greenish-gold, Rua and the guardian pulled away the thatch and let in the sunlight. Rua kindled a fire and set the house alight. The timber and the reeds in the walls flamed fiercely under the water until, by the steam and the flooding sunlight, the Ponaturi perished in their thousands.

While the fire cracked and roared, Rua tore away the carved bargeboards, the side posts, the ridgepole and the door and window frames of the house and swam with them to the beach. He drew them up on the dry land and set them in his own house to be an example to men for all time of the craftsmanship of wood-carving.

18

Kahukura and the Fairy Fisherman

Kahukura was a chief. He was not like other men, for his skin was fair like the sand on the beach below his pa. His hair was tinged with the copper-coloured glow of the sun, and in his wide-set eyes there was a look of something unearthly and far-seeing.

The old men of the tribe would talk about it in the low rumbling voice of aged warriors when the shadows were short on the ground and the young men were at work in the kumara plantations.

"See him now," said Tohe, the old fighting man with the bright scar that cut through the whorls of the moko on his cheek. "Now is the time when the old men see once again the days of their youth. When the time comes that we shall make the long journey to the Reinga, we shall see strange sights in our dreams. But Kahukura is young. What does he see over the Ocean of Kiwa that is hidden to our eyes?"

There was no movement amongst the men, but bright eyes looked over the busy pa and the tall palisade to the distant headland where a figure stood, black against the sky.

Kahukura was dreaming. His eyes were open and he stood with his feet firmly braced, facing the sea and the breakers that crashed on the rocks blow. A roller burst at the base of the cliff and spray hissed past him, but he made no movement. His spirit was wandering in the land of the far north, in the beautiful country of hill and forest, of river and sand, where the gulls wheel and cry and the spirits of the dead march steadily on to Te Reinga, to the giant pohutukawa tree that overhangs the Doorway of Death.

Time after time this dream had come to Kahukura, the dream of something waiting for him in the distant northland, something that

called to him, urging him to venture into that country where the
land ends and only the ocean surges await the warriors of Aotearoa.

The chief sighed and turned his back on the sea. When he was
old he would tread that path, with slaves to accompany him. But
before that time came he would go alone, while he was still young
and the breath of life was in his nostrils. As he walked back to the
pa he could see the young men examining their fishing lines and
sorting out the bone hooks. In Kahukura's coastal pa there were
many mouths to feed and the canoes went out in all weathers with
trailing lines so that their meals of fern-root and kumara, birds and
rats, might be varied with a tasty morsel of fish.

In the house of entertainment that night the young people
danced and played games while the old men and women looked on,
remembering the days of their youth when their bodies were
supple. Kahukura took no part in the dances. He sat in the corner
with unseeing eyes, for suddenly, in the midst of the laughter and
noise, a ghostly voice was sounding in his ears. "Go north, Kahukura," it said. "Go alone. Go to Rangiaowhia, to Rangiaowhia, to
Rangiaowhia."

When the games were over and his people lay silent on their
sleeping mats, Kahukura rose softly and stepped over the sleeping
forms. Only Tohe was awake. His bright eyes watched the departing
chief as he stood in the moonlight for a moment and then departed.
Tohe was wise. He said nothing, not even when the tribesmen made
their vain search for the missing chief in the morning. It had
seemed to him as though Kahukura knew what he was doing and
it was safer not to meddle.

Day after day Kahukura travelled north. He stopped only when
weariness overcame him. He took his rest in the shelter of rocks
and on mossy patches in the forest, and in the tall grasses. Sometimes the rain chilled him, and sometimes he walked under the hot
sun as it moved slowly across the heaven, held by the ropes with
which Maui and his brothers had tied it. Sometimes Marama, the
moon, looked down and smiled at the tiny figure that trudged on
so steadily towards the end of the land.

Kahukura came to a place where flax plants thrashed their long
leaves in the autumn winds. Some of them were knotted firmly
together and he knew that the souls of the dead were passing by. At

night he seemed to hear the thin cries of the departed ones, but above them rose the insistent whisper, "To Rangiaowhia."

Then came a night when he heard the voice no longer. There was a great emptiness of sound and the hissing of the waves on the sand was like an echo from a spirit world that had movement and life in it but scarcely any sound. Kahukura closed his eyes but sleep would not come to him. He shivered, for a faint music was coming across the water. It was coming nearer and he heard paddles and then voices laughing and singing. He looked across the beach and in the darkness he saw shining lights – the lights of the Turehu, the fair-skinned fairy folk of Aotearoa. Canoes were gliding on the water which broke into little dancing lights. The Turehu were fishing.

Kahukura remembered that in the half-light when he had thrown himself down to sleep that night, he had seen parts of fish lying on the beach, yet there had been no marks of human feet to show where the fishermen had been. This must be Rangiaowhia, the fishing ground of the fairy people.

He crept down to the water's edge. The friendly night hid him from their eyes. They were much closer to the shore now, and he heard them saying, "The net here! The net here!" He could not understand the words. What was the "net"? The only ways Kahukura knew of catching fish were by hook and line and spear. These were fairy words and this must be fairy magic.

The canoes drew closer to the shore. They were far apart, and in a great crescent between them was a gleaming line inside which were flashes of fire that darted to and fro in the darkness as the fish leapt from the water. The canoes touched the shore and the fairies sprang out. Kahukura could see that the strange bubbling line must be the net. The fish were jumping everywhere and he could hear the slap-slap of their bodies as they sprang out of the water and fell back again. The fairies were pulling the ends of the net. Kahukura came closer and mixed with them. His skin was fair like theirs, and in the darkness they did not notice that they were being helped by a mortal. Kahukura pulled at the flax rope. He felt wet knotted rushes passing through his hands.

There was a last rush of fairy people up the beach with Kahukura in the middle of them. The small crescent of net was live with a struggling mass of silver. In the meshes was a great haul of

The fairy net remained
in Kahukura's hands.

fish. The fairies dropped the end of the net and ran back to the water's edge.

They seized the flapping bodies and strung them on cords, each working by himself in haste lest the dawn should come before they finished. Kahukura strung his cords with fish, but he did not tie a knot at the end, so that when he lifted his string the fish slid off on to the sand. A fairy saw them falling and he dropped his own load and came to help Kahukura tie the knot properly. When he had gone, Kahu untied it again. Then he raised his load, and again the fish slid off. Another fairy came to his assistance.

Time and again he played this trick on the unsuspecting Turehu. He was watching the eastern sky. Far over the sea there was a faint tinge of light. It grew stronger until he could see the bushes above the beach and a big rock standing out of the sea like some guardian of the deep. The fairies were running to the canoes with their strings of fish, but still Kahu's fish dropped off his unknotted cord, and still the fairies helped him. The light was growing strong. The fish would all have been taken away had not Kahukura delayed the fairy people.

A bright beam of light shone over the ocean, lighting up the clouds. A cry of dismay rang out from the Turehu. At last they had seen that a man was with them. They rushed down the beach to their canoes, but they were too late. Tama-nui-te-Ra, the bright shining sun, was sending his rays over the long miles of ocean. The sand turned gold in the light. The fairies scattered and disappeared; the canoes shrank and crumbled until nothing remained but a few bundles of rushes and flax stalks. The fairy voices died away.

Kahukura stood alone on the shining beach. The fish were gone. Only one thing remained. In his hands were cords of flax tied in a strange pattern, and wet with sea water. He remembered the cry of the Turehu: "The net here!"

It was Tohe who was first to see him return, Tohe the wise who gave the greeting. "Welcome!" he said. "Chief who went forth in the night as one with a purpose, thou hast returned in the daylight, and as one who has fared far and gained rich treasure."

Kahu's eyes shone. Over his shoulder he carried a tangle of woven flax. The people had come at the call of Kahu, but they feared that his mind had left him, for in reply to their greetings, all he said was, "The net! The net!"

The young men took out the long nets that Kahu had taught them to make, for he had studied the tying of the knots as he journeyed home. Instead of a single fish flapping on the hook or on the barb of the spear, the young men now brought in a teeming harvest of fish, and there was plenty for rangatira and toa, for wives and sons and daughters and even for slaves.

This was the gift which Kahukura won from the fairy fishermen at Rangiaowhia in the long ago.

19

Whispering Ghosts
of the West

This is a story about the Aitanga-a-nuku-mai-tore, the half-human people amongst whom the venturesome Tura lived for a while.

Two friends, Pungarehu and Koko-muka-hau-nei, went fishing for barracouta. A sudden storm drove them out to sea. Day after day they were driven before the wind. When it dropped and the sea fell calm, their sail was torn to shreds and their provisions were nearly exhausted. Fortunately they soon came to a place where the water shallowed, and they reached a low-lying land.

They dragged the canoe ashore and looked for firewood so that they could dry their sodden clothing and warm their chilled bodies. They could find nothing but brambles and small bushes, but they were resourceful men. They took the wood from their fish-hooks and held it under their armpits to dry. Lighting a fire of twigs, they put the wood on it and cooked the little food they had left. Feeling refreshed, they set out to explore the country.

Presently they came across some peculiar footprints in soft earth. They seemed to have been made by a club-footed man who walked with the aid of a stick. Following the footprints they came to a forest and heard the sound of adzes. They crept forward and peeped through the undergrowth. The Aitanga were cutting down trees and lopping off the branches. Every time an adze bit into the wood and a chip flew into the air, the adze-wielder followed it with his eyes.

Pungarehu said to Koko-muka, "O man! The eyes of these people are watchful! We must be careful."

"They have not seen us yet in spite of their sharp eyes," he replied.

They crept along on their bellies like lizards, until they came to a place where one of the Aitanga was working by himself. Inching their way forward, they sprang to their feet. Punga grasped him round the waist and pulled him under the cover of the bushes, while Koko held his hand over his mouth to stifle his cries. When they were at a safe distance from the clearing they released him and sat down.

The Aitanga man looked at them with wondering eyes. "Where do you two come from?"

"Oh," said Punga airily, "We came from the interior on the wings of the wind."

The man looked at them steadily. "Where do you come from?"

Punga replied, "We have both come from Hawaiki, from far over the ocean, from a land unknown to you. Where do you live?"

"You must follow me and I will show you. Come back with me to my people."

They went to the clearing and met the other workers who crowded round them, touching their skins and feeling their clothes. Then they all set off down a forest path. One of the leaders came up to Punga and Koko and said, "We are getting close to our own settlement. You look friendly men, and I must give you a warning. If any of our people come up to you and begin to dance and grimace, take no notice of them. If you laugh at them they will kill you."

When they reached the settlement they saw the strange people in their tree-top houses. They climbed up to one of them and food was set before them. It was whale-meat, raw and putrid, which the Aitanga ate with relish. Punga and Koko managed to conceal their disgust, and put their uneaten portions away unobtrusively. They stayed talking to their hosts all afternoon, and for the evening meal the same fare was set before them.

They were taken to a larger house in another tree and the night's entertainment began. The dancers held ceremonial weapons made of flint and of wood with sharks' teeth inset. They began a peculiar dance and sang a verse which was a salutary warning to the visitors.

> *Now you laugh,*
> *Now you don't.*
> *Now you laugh,*
> *Now you don't.*

The verse was accompanied by vicious thrusts with the sharp flint and sharks' teeth weapons, and Punga and Koko had no difficulty in repressing their laughter.

By the following day they were faint with hunger. They kindled a fire and as the smoke drifted across, the people who had gathered in a large circle to see what these strange men were doing, broke into a chant.

> *Whispering ghosts of the west,*
> *Who brought you here*
> *To our land?*
> *Stand up and go.*

Punga and Koko took no notice. They dug a pit, placed the fire in it with stones on top, and when the heat shimmered up, they laid the food on green leaves and covered the oven.

When the oven was opened the delicious savour drew the circle closer. The whispering ghosts offered the food to the Aitanga, and suspicions were forgotten as everyone joined in the meal.

"You are our friends," they said. "You are kehua. You are powerful ghosts who have come to help us in our need."

"It is you who are ghosts," Pungarehu replied. "At least you are not men. How can we help you?"

"You are powerful ghosts," they repeated. "Help us, whispering ghosts of the west."

"What evil plagues you?" Pungarehu asked.

"It is the poua-kai, the man-eater. It is a bird which eats our people."

"Where does it live? Does it come to your village?"

"No, it lives by the river. When we go to bring water to quench our thirst it captures our people and carries them off."

"Can you see it coming?"

"Yes."

"Then we will try to help you. Take us to the place where it appears and help us build a house on the ground."

They crept down to the dark pool in the river in the early morning. While one or two bright stars remained to watch them they silently erected the beams, tying them with flax and weaving rushes for the walls and roof. There was no door and but a single window. Pungarehu and Koko-muka crept inside and told the Aitanga to go back to the village and send one of their number to draw water at daybreak.

They sat silently inside the house, shivering in the dank air and watching the stars pale and fade away. Bright shafts of light sprang across the sky and the birds began their dawn song.

Shuffling footsteps were heard and an old man appeared carrying a calabash down to the water. The dawn song stopped, and above the gurgling of the water in the calabash Punga and Koko heard the slow beating of wings. The poua-kai appeared above the tree-tops, a dark shadow against the rising sun. It swooped down and a gust of foetid air washed over the house. Its ugly neck was stretched out, and as the giant bird passed the window of the house, its beak was thrust out like the sharp, pointed tongue of the father of taiahas. Pungarehu leaned out of the window and struck a heavy blow with his stone axe, shattering the creature's wing. The bird fell sideways, its beak jabbing and its eyes peering at the flimsy house but failing to discover its hidden enemies. It turned in a half circle and Koko-muka, seizing his opportunity, struck the other wing, leaving the bird helpless on the ground.

The two friends sprang lightly through the window. They leaped over the flailing claws, escaped the sharp beak and battered it to death. The old man raised a quivering cry of triumph and the Aitanga flocked down to see their dead enemy, some dancing round it with derisive gestures and others going boldly to its lair to marvel at the huge pile of human bones, and to wonder at the audacity of the whispering ghosts of the west.

Had Punga and Koko wished to remain they might have lived like atuas for the rest of their days, but as Tura had discovered, the Aitanga were alien in thought to men. They began to think of their homes, of their wives and children, and of the pleasant hour that comes after the evening meal on the marae when men and women share the gossip of the day and the young people entertain with dance and song.

They went back to their canoe, repaired the damage that had been done by the storm and left the shores of a land that could never be home, to return to their own country.

There was no one to meet them when they beached the canoe.

The giant bird lay helpless
on the ground.

They shouted but their cry was forlorn like the lonely call of a gull. They went to their houses, but grass and weeds were grown thickly round them, the walls looked old and were broken in places, and when they went inside there was a musty smell that comes from disuse.

"We have grown old!" Pungarehu whispered, "and our families are dead!"

They went outside. At some distance there was another house and a wisp of smoke curled out of the opening in the roof. They tiptoed towards it, pulled the door open softly, and crept inside. Many families were lying there, and there was comforting warmth and the smell of friendly people. They crept from group to group looking into the faces of the sleepers.

Pungarehu bent over a woman with a familiar face She stirred in her sleep and murmured:

> *As evening comes*
> *My love returns*
> *I hear his voice*
> *Far distant*
> *Beyond the mountain peak*
> *And sundering seas*
> *Where echoes vainly call.*

When morning came and the sun poked its inquiring fingers through the doorway and window, the sleepers woke up and saw two strangers lying by the ashes of the fire.

Two women went over to them. One said to the other, "They are our first husbands whom we thought had died long ago. They have returned to us in all their youth and manhood."

The old women stood with hands clasped and with tears streaming down their wrinkled faces and dropping on the ashes of the dead fire.

20

Peha and the Goblins

Peha-ane-tonga picked his way through the undergrowth, staring up at the tall trees. He was in search of a strong totara for the sternpiece of his canoe. He found what he was looking for in a little shadowed glade. Taller trees hemmed in the one he had selected, but there was plenty of room to swing his axe. He sat down on a fallen log and looked at the tree critically. Yes, he could see the sternpiece taking shape in his mind, flowering into an invisible tracery of delicate curves and whorls. Then his face clouded over. He remembered his enemy Parukau of the river pa. Parukau was skilled in magic arts and a dangerous man to have for an enemy, but he was low-born. Peha had heard that he had been boasting, telling his people that his canoe would be the best on the coast when he had finished it.

He stood up and brushed Parukau from his mind. He grasped his axe-handle firmly. The greenstone blade bit into the solid wood, but there it remained! Peha stood petrified. A horrid screech had come from the tree. He listened but the forest was silent again. The birds were still and even the wind in the trees had died away so that the leaves stood stiff and motionless as if waiting for something to happen. The air was cold on his body. He realised at once that he must be standing on sacred ground.

Then it happened! A hollow, mocking laugh rang through the glade. He turned round, his keen eyes searching the undergrowth, but no one was there. Again came the jeering laughter, and he looked up into the tree. He recoiled in horror. A few feet above him, on the bare branch of a tree, was a round, hairless face. It was alive, for the skin crinkled and the eyes closed to a slit as it laughed again. Only the head was there, resting on the limb of a tree, without body, arms or legs to support it.

Peha recited incantations and called on his ancestors for help.

Peha stared at the face in horror.

Presently he felt the blood running warm in his veins once more and lost his fear of the ghostly head. But no sooner did he touch his axe than the unearthly shriek rang out again. This time it was followed by mocking laughter which came from every side – not one laugh, but many. The voices came nearer until they seemed to be but a few inches away and he was almost deafened by the sound. A chip of wood rose from the ground, lifted by invisible fingers. It was jerked backwards and then launched at him like a dart. It glanced off his shoulder, and was followed by a rain of chips and splinters of wood which came from every direction, while the grinning face still stared at him from the branch and the weird laughter rose and fell around him. A sharp piece of wood struck him in the face and he felt the blood running down his cheek.

Then the fighting spirit rose in Peha. Seizing a stout branch which lay by the tree, he swung it round his head. A hoot of laughter sounded in his ears. He dashed the rude club with all his might in the direction of the laugh. It stopped at once and gave place to a moan, while he felt the club check and sink into flesh that could not be seen. He laid about him, hearing the dull thud of wood on bone and flesh, feeling the tingling in his fingers. The laughter died away and presently he knew he was alone, save for the head which nodded and blinked at him from the tree.

Peha picked up his axe and made his way out of the forest. He heard the laughter again, but more faintly. But the head accompanied him, leaping from tree to tree, jumping ahead and falling behind, with its eyes fixed on him all the while.

He heaved a sigh of relief as the trees thinned out and he came out on to the open plain. In the distance lay his own village and beyond it the river pa where Parukau lived. Just in front of him was an old deserted pa which had been used for many years as a burying place.

The head gave a whoop and sped past him, nearly brushing him so that he felt the cold wind of its passing. It hung over the graveyard for a moment and then plunged into the ground which opened to receive it, closing over it again.

Peha still had his club in his hand. He hurried to the graveyard, climbed the weather-worn ramparts and began to turn the soil over, using his club as a ko. Presently he came upon the body of a man standing upright but buried under the earth. He dug round the body in the soft soil until it was free and could be lifted out.

"This is a device of the tipua," thought Peha. "I am not a slave to be deceived by this foolishness."

The lifeless figure stood stiffly on its feet. Peha stepped back and hit it with his club. The outline of the man wavered and changed as he watched. There seemed to be something familiar about it. Peha stared in bewilderment. The man he had drawn out of the ground was no longer there; he had changed into the form of Parukau, his enemy of the river pa. Parukau looked at him and then turned and ran into the gathering dusk. Peha felt an added strength surge into him.

The following day he went down to the river pa. He saw Parukau in the distance but took no notice of him. When night came he joined the others in the big whare.

"Why do you come to visit us here, Peha-ane-tonga?" the chief asked. "Are you tired of your own place?"

Peha sprang to his feet and strode to the end of the house between the lines of men and women and returned to the foot of the post where he had been sitting.

"In the forest I began to cut down a tree. The place was haunted ..." His eyes flashed fire as he told the tale of his adventure. "Now why do you think I have come to your pa, O Chief?"

The chief beckoned to him, "Stand by me, Peha, son of warriors," he said. 'Parukau is but the husk of a man. His mana has entered into you. You have the spirit of two men."

Peha left the house, passing Parukau who sat sulking by the doorway, and strode up the hill to his own pa, fearless of the spirits and ghosts that haunt the darkness, for he had the strength of two men. The spirit of Parukau had joined itself to the spirit of Peha-ane-tonga.

21

Stories of Taniwha

Aotearoa is peopled with taniwha and ngarara, strange monsters of land and water. The white man's magic has sent them to sleep, but they lie hidden under hills and deep water. Every tribe has its story of these man-eating monsters, so we must remember that the tales that are related here are the tales of night-time, told by the old men of the tribe when the children are asleep and firelight flickers on the reed walls of the whare and the darkness becomes alive with strange things out of the past.

Here are tales for a single night; but the stories of taniwha are endless, like the nights of a man's lifetime.

The Lizard Taniwha

Ah, you would have shuddered to see Kaiwhakaruaki. His skin was damp and bleached from living in the dark cave in the forest. When he dragged his repulsive body over the ground, even the birds flew away. While searching for food one day, he surprised a woman in the forest. Ignoring her screams, he dragged her to his cave and kept her there as his wife. He had no fear of losing her, for when he entered the cave his body blocked the entrance, and when he left it he tied a long rope of flax to her hair and held the other end. From time to time he pulled the rope to make sure that she was still there.

As the day passed the woman spent all her time planning how to escape. She could not outrun the monster and her freedom could only be won by guile. At length she thought of a plan and put it into operation at the first possible moment.

When Kai left the cave to go in search of food, she went outside and cut the rope that bound her hair with a sharpened shell. Holding the end of the severed rope in her hands, she tied it to a young sapling. In the distance she heard the taniwha crashing through the trees while the startled birds flew overhead.

The taniwha was lured
into the whare.

Presently the rope jerked tight. The sapling bent to the strain and straightened itself again. She held her breath for a long minute. Then she heard the taniwha going further away, and she knew that she was safe.

She hurried straight to her village and told her story to her friends, who resolved to make an end of the taniwha. The men worked at the building of a house big enough to take the gross body of Kaiwhakaruaki. When it was finished they sent one of the young men into the forest to invite the taniwha to come and live with them.

He went cautiously into the forest, shouted his invitation at the top of his voice, and ran back to the kainga.

Everyone was seated on the marae, anxiously watching the forest where it crept up to the nearest whare. In a little while the bushes were pushed aside and Kaiwhakaruaki came out. The little children hid their heads on their mothers' breasts, and even the warriors edged backwards as the horrible beast waddled forward, his head over-topping the whares, his eyes gleaming like the embers of a fire.

"Where is my wife?" he asked in a hoarse voice.

The woman stepped forward boldly, putting the toas to shame.

"Do not fear, Kaiwhaka," she said gently. 'It is I, your wife."

"Why have you run away?"

"I grew weary of the cold and damp in your cave," she said. "This is my home, but you must come here to live with me. See, the men of my tribe have built a house for us."

Kaiwhakaruaki turned his head and looked at the huge whare that had just been built. He seemed satisfied and said, "At first I thought you had turned into a tree, but if this is where you are, I will remain."

He thrust up his head and looked at the people. "See that I am well fed," he said. "The anger of Kaiwhakaruaki is to be feared. Now I go to sleep. Send my wife to me," and he lumbered into the whare.

"Now is the time," the woman whispered. "You know what to do!"

They piled brushwood and manuka against the walls of the house.

"Where is my wife?" Kai rumbled. "Send her to me for it is growing dark."

While the pile of wood grew higher, they took a piece of timber, dressed it in the woman's clothes, and thrust it through the door, closing it again quickly The woodpile was soon finished. The chief thrust a torch into it and the fire took hold of the dry twigs and ran through the brushwood, crackling and leaping to life in the darkness.

They heard Kai turn over, for the earth shook under their feet. "What is the noise that I hear?" he called.

"Hush, it is the wind roaring in the tree-tops," they shouted. "A storm is coming up."

By now the walls of the whare were ablaze and Kai realised that he had been tricked. He rushed to and fro in his narrow prison but the flames drove him back until, as the rafters sank slowly inwards and a gout of flame rushed up to the sky, he died.

But not the whole of Kaiwhaka was killed. His tail escaped. Falling from his body, it wriggled under the blazing wood and escaped to the forest, where its children live to this very day in the form of the moko papa, the little tree lizard.

Ah, it is another story that is true, for do not these little descendants of the tail of Kaiwhakaruaki have the power to lose their tails without hurt to themselves?

The Taniwha of Waikaremoana

Waikaremoana, loveliest of lakes, sea of rippling waters, lies placidly now under the summer skies, but in the far-off days there came the pokaretanga (agitation) that gave to this moana, this little sea, its name.

Mahu was thirsty. He told his daughter, Hau-mapuhia, to go to the spring and bring him water. Hau refused to go, and although Mahu shouted at her she remained stubborn, and in the end he had to go himself.

As he bent over the water he felt his anger mounting. His other children had disobeyed him and had been turned into stones, but a worse fate would befall Hau. He stayed by the lake until nightfall. Presently he heard footsteps. It was Hau, searching for her father. When she came close to him he stepped from behind a bush and thrust her into the water. The girl sank down until the water closed over her head. Mahu pressed down on her until her struggles ceased. Then he left the lake and went straight to the sea.

Hau was not dead. She lost the soft rounded form of a young woman. Her hands turned into fish-like fins and her legs were joined together. Her body was covered with scales, her face became ugly and her long hair turned into straggling waterweed. For a while she lay still on the bottom of the lake. Then the cold blood stirred in her and she swept out into deep water. Hau had become a taniwha.

There was little room for her to move in the tiny lake. She plunged into the earth and forced her way through the rocks, thrusting hills aside, shouldering the soil from her as the point of the ko turns the kumara patch. She was stopped only by the great Huiarau Range that stood across her path. The water rushed into the channel she had carved, but she turned and swam through it and attacked the land to the east. She was foiled again, but she hurled herself at the outlet of the lake at Te Wharawhara. While she struggled the arms of the lake extended in her wake and the waters tossed and rippled in the shallows.

Far away she could hear the murmur of the Ocean of Kiwa, and she struggled frantically in her narrow bed.

Foot by foot she crept forward, threshing the water and crying in the unaccustomed voice of a taniwha. Mahu heard her and sent her fish to satisfy her hunger – fish that still swim in placid Waikaremoana. When she had eaten she was still hungry, and Mahu sent her shellfish, which remain embedded in the rocks from that far-off day to this. Then the sun rose and Hau-mapuhia the taniwha lay still in death with the waters of the lake running down her body and her hair trailing in the rippling waters.

The Pakeha sees her as a rock, but the Maori knows better. She is Hau-mapuhia the taniwha who made the winding waterways of Waikaremoana, made them ripple during the long night of her struggle for the freedom of the wide-spreading Ocean of Kiwa.

The Pet Taniwha

Tu-ariki went from Rangitikei to Whakatu (Nelson) on a fishing excursion. When the canoes were in deep water Tu-ariki caught a young shark. As it threshed about in the bottom of the canoe, Tu-ariki was attracted by the fish. It seemed different from other sharks. The look in its eyes was almost friendly. All the way back to Whakatu it lay on the floorboards looking at him in such a way that Tu-ariki could not bear to kill it.

As soon as the canoe was beached he picked it up in his arms. The shark lay still and allowed him to carry it along the shore to the rocks where there was a deep pool, fringed with great boulders. Tu-ariki slid the fish into the pool. It swam slowly round the circle of rocks and then came to the side where Tu stood, nosing the bank.

Every day Tu-ariki came and fed it. The shark swam to him and would not leave him until he left. By the time the fishermen were ready to return to Rangitikei, Tu-ariki had grown fond of his fish and could not bear to be parted from it, so he took it with him and released it in the river.

"Why do you keep Tutae-poroporo?" his people asked him. Everyone knew Tutae-poroporo, Tu's pet shark.

"As the kuri is to the kiwi-hunter, so is this shark to me," said Tu.

With constant feeding Tutae-poroporo grew as big as a whale and nearly filled the river. But it was not like a whale, nor yet like a shark, and it dawned on Tu that Tutae-poroporo was really a taniwha.

One day a war-party came to Rangitikei from Whanganui and Tu-ariki was killed and eaten. That night Tutae-poroporo waited for his master, but he did not come. All night the taniwha was restless. When morning came and Tu-ariki still did not come, Tutae-poroporo heaved his monstrous body out of the river and explored the paths that Tu had travelled. He could smell the man-scent strong upon them and he roamed to and fro, breaking trees and crushing plants, searching everywhere but in vain.

In his grief he plunged into the river and floated with it until he reached the sea. As he felt the waves under him he lifted his head out of the water, turning it from side to side and sniffing the breeze. To the north there was nothing; in the west there was only the clean sent of the open sea; to the south, ah, from the south the blood smell came heavy and strong. With a flick of his tail he turned round and sped south until he reached the Whanganui. There the smell was stronger still and his heart raged in his body. He swam up the river until he reached a deepwater pool, and there he made his home under the shadow of Tau-maha-aute.* He was no longer Tutae-poroporo the gentle pet of Tu-ariki; he was Tutae-poroporo, the scourge of the Whanganui. No canoe ever passed his hiding place. As soon as the paddles echoed through the walls of the canyon, Tutae rose from the river bottom and swallowed the travellers.

At first the Whanganui people knew nothing of the taniwha up-river, but soon there were so many canoes missing that they sent out search parties. When they discovered the truth of the man-eating monster they fled from their pas.

Then Tama-ahua, he who owned the magic feather,† flew to his pa at Waitotara and pleaded with a famous taniwha-killer, Ao-kehu by name. "The land is desolate because of the taniwha," he said. "Children mourn their fathers and wives their husbands."

"I shall come," said Ao-kehu.

A few days later he arrived with seventy of his people, bringing with him his two taniwha-killing weapons, Tai-timu and Tai-paroa, which were shaped like saws with sharks' teeth set in their edges.

Without wasting time, Ao-kehu set his people to making a box with a close-fitting lid, long enough to hold him and his weapons. The box was taken up-stream. Ao-kehu got into it with Tai-timu and Tai-paroa and the lid was closed and lashed firmly. Clay was pressed into the holes and cracks in the wood to make everything airtight, and the box was carried to the water and floated down the river.

As it came to Tau-maha-aute, Tutae-poroporo smelt the man-scent. The people, watching from the ridge which faced the cliff, saw Tutae-poroporo rise from the water like some great weather-worn rock. His mouth opened and engulfed the floating box, and then he was gone with nothing to tell of his passing except the waves that boiled under the rocks.

Crouched in his narrow box, Ao-kehu repeated incantations to the gods. He felt the sudden plunge as the box was swallowed and

---

* Well known to the Pakeha as Shakespeare Cliff.
† See page 219.

Ao-kehu escaped from the taniwha's body.

the taniwha sank to the bottom of the river. Lifting up his weapons, he sawed through the lid of the box and attacked the taniwha's body from the inside. The monster hurled himself from side to side and Ao-kehu was thrown about in the dark body, but after a final flurry, the taniwha fell on its side and died.

Presently the waiting people saw its body drifting down the river and they followed it till it came ashore. Setting to work at once, they cut it open and released Ao-kehu, and then removed the bodies of the people the taniwha had killed, and gave them decent burial.

Tutae-poroporo they left as food for the birds, and everyone rejoiced at its death. But in his home in the dim underworld perhaps Tu-ariki knew and grieved for the passing of a faithful friend.

22

Stories of the Moon and Stars

Rona and the Moon*

Rona and his wife and three children lived by some flat, damp land near a warm spring in the Kaipara district. They were not happy together, and after a quarrel, Rona's wife left him and went to live with her own people in the Paeroa sandhills, leaving the children with her husband.

Because he was only a man, Rona did not know how to look after his children properly. One night the children began to cry out asking for water. Rona had forgotten to bring it to the whare while it was daylight. The children kept crying, "O Rona, some water! We want some water to drink!" till the father grew tired of hearing their voices.

He got up from his mat and took up a calabash in each hand, but like a thoughtless, stupid man, he did not take a fire-brand to wave about and light up the path. As he went towards the spring he struck his foot against the root of a tree which grew in the path and hurt himself. A second time he struck his foot. He sat down and held his foot in his hand to ease the pain. He could still hear his children crying, "O Rona, some water!" He looked up into the sky and saw the stars, but they did not shine brightly enough to show the path.

The pain had made him bad-tempered, and he shouted, "Cooked-head moon!" which was a very bad curse. "Where are you now, cooked-head moon? You have left me in darkness so that I will

---

* Rona is usually spoken of as a woman. This version of the story is adapted from *Revenge*, by John White, edited by A.W. Reed.

The moon pulled Rona
away from the earth.

kill my feet with stumps and stones. Cooked-head moon for not showing light to me!"

He stood up and went on down the path, but the moon had heard his curse. He left his place in the sky and rushed to the earth. Before Rona had time to run, he was seized by the moon and swung up into the air. As he felt his feet leaving the ground he put both calabashes into his left hand and grasped the thick branch of a ngaio tree to try and hold himself down. His struggles were in vain. The moon dragged him away, and as Rona held fast, the ngaio was pulled up by the roots.

The children kept crying for water and even at that great distance Rona could hear them. Parched with thirst, they had come out of the house and called, "O Rona, where are you? Where are you? You are a long time getting the water!"

Rona called from his place in the moon, "I am up here with the stars and the moon. No water here! Here I am, up above!"

The children looked up and stared at the moon, but it had nearly reached its place in the sky and Rona's voice grew fainter and fainter until they could hear him no longer. They were afraid to go and get the water themselves. The next day they went to their mother and told her how their father had cursed the moon and was now up in the sky, where he would have to stay for ever. The mother came back to her old home with the children and took another husband; but she never said an angry word to him for fear that Rona and the moon would come some night and take him away too.

While she lived with her new husband she would not go out of her house in the nights of the moon, especially at the time of rakaunui, for then Rona and his calabashes and the ngaio could be seen in the moon.

The Little Eyes

The seven bright shining stars which are know to the Pakeha as the Pleiades have been known and loved by people of many lands. The ancient Greeks called them the Daughters of Atlas and Pleione; the Australian Aborigines knew them as Seven Sisters. The Maori people looked up and pointed out these stars to their children and told them that they were the left eyes of seven great chiefs.

Throughout the islands of the southern seas the Pleiades were always welcome, and when they first appeared in the west the new year began with feasting and dancing and the singing of songs.

There is a story about these seven stars which comes, not from Maoriland, but from another island in the Pacific. It is told here because it is about the ancient gods of Maoriland.

Once upon a time there was one star which shone so brightly that other stars dared not go near it lest their own beauty should be dimmed in its radiance. Like another moon it matched the beauty of all the other stars together so that the living things of earth loved it and waited nightly for it to light everything with its soft radiance.

Far up in the hills there was a tiny lake that loved this star. The hot day passed slowly until the star rose in the western sky. Then the lake shivered a little as it saw the beauty of the star. All through the night it mirrored the star in its calm waters.

One day the little lake was drowsing through the sunny hours when it heard the voice of Tane. You will remember that long before, Tane had brought all the stars in the Basket of the Milky Way and had scattered them over the blue robe of the Sky-father. Tane had become jealous of this star that had become so much brighter than the Shining Ones he had given to Rangi, and he planned to destroy it.

The little lake had overheard Tane's plan. All that night it watched the star and longed to tell it of the danger that threatened it. When Hine-ata, the Dawn Girl, rose and the sun shone on the lake, it whispered its secret to Rangi. The Sky-father was angry. He was powerless against Tane, but he caused the sun to shine fiercely on the waters of the lake until they dissolved in mist and rose above the earth. The wind carried the mist on its back far above the mountains until it reached the star, shining again in beauty with the coming of night. The misty lake waters rolled round the star until its light was dimmed.

When Tane and his followers came sweeping down the sky, the star was prepared. It fled through the heavens. All through the night Tane gained slowly on the star until, as the Shining Ones paled before the growing light, in desperation it fled to the highway of Tane, hoping to hide its light within the light. Then Tane snatched a Shining One from Rangi's canopy and flung it at the star. There was a crash that reverberated through the heavens and the star broke into pieces. Tane scooped them up in his hand and flung them away.

But where he threw them so carelessly they can still be found. The Little Eyes, men call them. Matariki is the Maori name – Little Eyes that men love, that twinkle for ever in the silent heavens.

The Shining Ones Who Fall From Their Places

Whanau-marama is the name the Maoris give to the stars. It means the Children of Light, but sometimes they are known as Ra Ririki, the little suns. We, who know so much about the universe in which we live, should remember that many years ago, when our fathers thought the world was flat and that the sun moved round the earth, some Maori thinker looked up into the clear night sky and wondered. He saw the twinkling lights that starred the robe of Rangi, shining down through endless space. He felt they were more than the playful children of Uru and, wiser than he knew, he called them the "little suns".

But the laughing children, the busy mothers and the fierce warrior fathers had no time to think thoughts as deep as these. They could see Tane busily scattering the Children of Light over his father's body. They saw the long, softly shining basket that stretches over Rangi's body and guards the little Shining Ones. They saw the Children of Light playing together as they did long ago at the foot of Maunganui. The Children pushed and scrambled together, and every now and then one of them tumbled out of the folds of Rangi's robe and fell in a long flash of light across the sky.

When we see a meteor fall towards the earth and burst into flame as it rushes through the heavy air, we say, "There is a shooting star." The Maori looks at it and thinks of the Child of Light who has fallen out of the garments of the sky as he played with his brothers and sisters.

Shining Lights of the South

In the far north the sky is sometimes lit by that strange phenomenon, the aurora borealis. In the south, when the cold polar light wrinkles and gleams far away, we call it the aurora australis.

The Maori called it Tahu-nui-a-Rangi – Glowing-big-of-Rangi – the great glowing of the sky.

A thousand years ago, when the Maoris sailed their canoes between Hawaiki and Aotearoa, some bold sailors went even further south, down to the land of unending snow and ice. There they stayed and while the long years have passed, still they remain in that bleak, unfriendly land. Sometimes they remember the warmth of their island homes and they light great fires which shine across the seas and light up all the southern sky. Then the Maori, looking out of his whare, sees that cold glow and in his musical language he calls it Tahu-nui-a-Rangi – The Great Glowing of the Sky.

There was another famous explorer who was mystified by the pulsating lights that glowed on the southern horizon. Was it indeed a fire that lit up the dark curtains of the cold, far away lands? Tamarereti wondered. He supervised the construction of a large ocean-going canoe made from a single totara tree, with tall topsides and beautifully carved prow and stern pieces, inlaid with iridescent paua shell, and with long plumes of brightly coloured feathers. When it was finished Tamarereti named it Te Rua-o-Maahu. Young men in the first flush of manhood volunteered for the hazardous journey. Reti chose a crew of seventy toas, and two tohungas who were noted for their wisdom and knowledge of the ceremonies needed for the protection and propitiation of the gods. Reti set sail for the south, guided by the stars of the Southern Cross. He sailed on until the sun was left behind and only the stars remained to comfort the sailors, and the pulsating ribbons of light to intimidate them. At length they heard the sound of breakers thundering against a rock-bound coast, and as they drew nearer their way was barred by cliffs of ice. Ice pinnacles were silhouetted against the radiance of the aurora australis, which Tamarereti named Nga Kurakura-o-Hine-nui-o-te-po, the sun splendours of the great lady of the night.

For a while the canoe cruised up and down the line of cliffs looking for a place to land while the air crackled with fire and a sound as of burning flax. Nowhere could they find a place to land. They ate the sea-food of that place, and while eating a tiny fish which had been taken from the stomach of a larger fish, Reti choked and died. "It was a small fish which choked Tamarereti," says an old proverb. It was a sad day for his men when they embalmed the body of their leader and began the long voyage back to Aotearoa.

The watchers in Reti's village had almost given up hope of seeing Te Rua-o-Maahu, but one stormy night they saw it driven towards them by the waves. The people gathered quickly on the shore, but the canoe struck a rock and was overturned. The bodies were washed ashore and anxiously examined by friends and relatives. One, badly mangled by the sharp rocks, was the body of Tamarereti. The spark of life remained in only two of the sailors, and even then but fitfully. A young man, and one of the tohungas, lived long enough to tell of their privations and discoveries in the ice-bound seas.

When the broken canoe was washed ashore the people filled it with brushwood and logs of firewood. The bodies of the dead voyagers were placed in it in a sitting position, as if they were still alive and presided over by Tamarereti, who was dressed in his finest cloak, holding a treasured weapon in his dead hand. At nightfall a torch was applied to the brushwood and the last long voyage was taken by the men who had given their lives in search of the fires of the Lady of Death.

The canoe lives on for ever in the night sky. The stars that the Pakeha calls the Southern Cross are the paua shell-studded prow of the canoe, "the little jewel-casket of Tamarereti". The Milky Way, lying huge and vast across the heavens, is the canoe itself, Te Waka-o-Tamarereti, with the star Au-tahi (Canopus) adorning the stern-post. The pointers of the Southern Cross are the anchor rope, and the starless gulch sometimes known as the Dark Hole is the anchor stone of the canoe of Tamarereti.

How the Moon was Made

Long ago before the path to the underworld was closed to mortals, two women were filled with curiosity about what went on in the Rarohenga. They filled kits with dried kumara, and made the long journey to the Reinga. They descended the roots of the ancient pohutukawa and cautiously lowered themselves through the sea-weed. They found themselves in darkness in a cave which ran far under the earth. Feeling their way with their hands, they went on until they saw a light in the distance, small and faint like a glow-worm.

As they drew nearer the glow expanded and they saw that it was a fire, round which three old, grey-haired spirits were crouching.

"It is a spirit fire," one of the women whispered. "If we can take some it will warm our homes for ever, but I dare not go any closer."

The other was bolder. She walked up to the old men who gazed at her in astonishment. While they were still startled she put the basket of kumara in front of them and snatched a burning log from the fire.

The women ran back towards the Reinga with the old men close at their heels. At first they thought that they had escaped, but as they came to the surface of the water, one of the spirits caught the heel of the woman who was carrying the burning brand. In a panic she threw the log away and managed to drag herself free.

In the terror of the moment fear had lent strength to her arm. The blazing wood flew high into the air – up and up until it caught in Rangi's robe, where it glows steadily for ever as Marama the moon.

We have never been able to learn all the star-lore of the Maori, and now it is too late. In olden days he watched for the rising and setting of the stars, he planted his crops when they were favourable, and guided his canoes by them on his long ocean voyages. He loved the beautiful Children of Light, the Ra Ririki of the Southern Hemisphere.

23

Stories of Birds

The Great Bird of Ruakapanga

Te Manu Nui a Ruakapanga was the name the Maoris gave to the moa, and the Great Bird of Ruakapanga was the meaning of the name. Ages have passed since the moa stalked over our hills and plains, but in the days of long ago there were many of these long-legged children of Tane.

Ruakapanga was one of the first men to come to Aotearoa. He roved through the bush in the Bay of Plenty district with his companions, hunting the wild birds and living on berries and fernroot, until one day he espied in the distance the huge birds which might well have hunted him. Ruakapanga and his friends had never seen such a sight before. On the canoe voyage from Hawaiki they may have seen whales, but they had never dreamed that such huge creatures lived on land.

Conquering the fear in his heart, Ruakapanga prepared a trap for the moas. He and his friends worked diligently, twisting and plaiting vines to hold the giants. The trap was baited and when, after much watching, a moa ventured inside, a shout of triumph arose from Rua and his men, but they had shouted too soon. With its tree-like legs the moa kicked and slashed at the vines until they were tossed aside, and it strode away. Rua patiently baited the mended trap again, but his next moa escaped as easily as the first. Many times he snared a moa, but each time it escaped.

Then Rua called his men together and they fashioned a trap that even Paraoa the whale might have despaired of breaking. When an unsuspicious moa walked into it and turned in anger at the shouts of the hunters, it found it could not fight its way to freedom. The spears of the warriors were soon buried in its body and it died.

So Pouakai, which we know as moa, and the scientist as Dinornis, was called the Great Bird of Ruakapanga, the dauntless hunter.

Pou and the Great Bird

Pou-rangahua the strong, who lived at Turanga where Gisborne
now stands, had a little boy whom he loved greatly. Anything that
his baby's hands reached for, Pou-rangahua was ready to procure at
any cost. As his son grew older, Pou noticed that he was always
putting out his tongue, and always in the same direction. When he
was lying down he would roll over to poke out his tongue, and
when he was standing he would turn round so that it would point
in the same way.

Pou talked it over with his wife and they decided that the little
boy was hungry, and he was pointing in the direction where he
knew there was good food.

"Then I'll find it for him," said Pou-rangahua the strong. He
girded himself with his weapons, took some food with him and
pushed his canoe into the breakers. His wife watched him as he
paddled away. She saw the muscles standing out on his broad back
as he swung the paddle. She saw the canoe, looking small and lonely,
growing smaller every minute, and the flash of the paddle-blade as
it reflected the sunlight at every stroke. Then the canoe was only a
tiny speck; then it was lost to sight. Pou-rangahua was facing the
countless leagues of open sea to find food for his son.

Over the endless plains of ocean he sailed, day after day, until at
last the canoe grated on the beach of a distant country. Pou leaped
ashore, glad to feel the firm ground under his feet. He soon made
friends with the people of the land, and they shared their evening
meal with him. He cried out in delight as he tasted the steaming
vegetables in the basket they put before him. It was sweeter than
any fern root he had ever eaten. It was the kumara. Pou had never
even heard of it before. It did not grow in the long bright land he
had come from, and he knew at once that this was the food for
which his son was craving.

He stayed in the new country for a while, but all the time he
longed to be back in his own home at Turanga and to see his son's
face when he tasted the kumara. Alas! Pou's canoe had gone.
Perhaps the storm had battered it to pieces on the shore; perhaps
the tide had gently lifted it until it floated away. Pou had no means
of returning to his own home.

The ariki Tane was his friend and that night, as they lay side by side on their sleeping mats, while Pou looked at the same bright stars that shone over his home in far-away Turanga, he told his troubles to Tane. Tane raised himself on his elbow.

"There is only one way," he said. "It is a dangerous way, but a man who seeks his home after long journeying thinks little of danger."

"I have faced dangers, and been in peril of the waters as I sailed the Ocean of Kiwa," said Pou. "What greater dangers could I find than the peril that is in the sea, when I had only a hollowed log between me and the endless waters?"

"You were in peril then," Tane agreed, "and you will be in peril on your return. You must travel on the back of the great bird of Ruakapanga."

Pou clenched his hands until the knuckles showed white under the dark skin.

"Te Manu nui a Ruakapanga," he whispered. "But how will he take me, O friend?"

"I have said there will be dangers," replied Tane. "You may mount on his back if you dare, and hold closely to him. He will carry you swiftly to your home. Half-way there, on a high hill called Hikurangi, which rises from the deep ocean, lives Tama the Ogre. Of him you must beware, for if you fall into his clutches, your strength will not help you."

"How can I avoid the monster?"

"You must wait until the sun is setting. Just before it sinks into the ocean the level rays will blind the ogre, and if you are bold, you may fly past before he can catch you."

Early the next morning Pou-rangahua took two baskets and mounted on the back of the moa. In those days the great bird of Ruakapanga could fly. It beat its wings and lifted Pou and his heavy load without effort. Flapping its wings lazily, it headed south. Pou looked down and saw the tiny figures of his friends far below. On a cliff nearby Tane was standing, shading his eyes as he watched Pou begin his perilous flight.

As many miles as Pou had travelled in a day in his canoe he now covered in an hour, and as the sun began its swift tropic descent, he sighted the hill Hikurangi. Pou tugged at the moa's neck and it flew more slowly until the lower edge of the sun touched the sea. Then

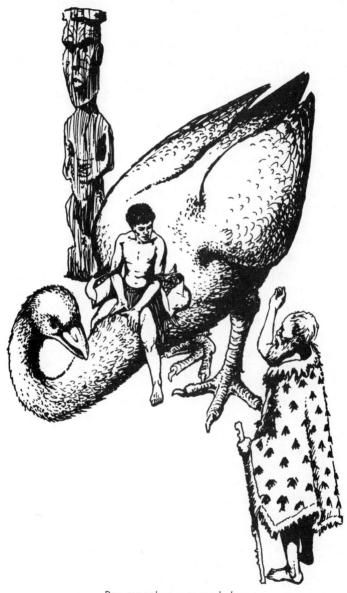

Pou-rangahua was ready for
the homeward journey.

in a blinding glory of light they sped past the hill. There was a roar when Tama heard the beating of giant wings, but before he could see them they had passed, and the danger was over.

When the shores of Aotearoa came in sight, Pou's heart leaped at the thought of seeing his wife and child again, and of the joy they would find in his treasure. In his eagerness to reach home he was guilty of two evil deeds. First he plucked two of the feathers of the moa, and this was a grievous sin. Then he forced the moa to carry him right to his home. Tane had warned him to descend as soon as he reached his own country, but Pou was anxious to get home, and in his eagerness he was selfish, as men sometimes are.

Great was the welcome that Pou received, and great his gift to Aotearoa, for in every pa and kainga men have cause to bless Pou-rangahua and the new food he brought to Turanga.

Far over the sea the days passed slowly as Tane looked in vain for the bird he had lent to Pou. It had been detained too long and Tama of Hikurangi caught it with his spells in the hot noonday and destroyed it.

Te Manu nui a Ruakapanga is dead. Only fragments of giant eggshells and bones remind us of him – only these and his tiny brother the kiwi, and a leaning rata tree which we may see and chance to remember that it was trampled on by a moa long years ago.

Hokioi and the Hawk

When the sun has departed and Marama the moon is swallowed up by the clouds, when the firelight gleams on the pillars of the house and the talk and laughter have died away, sometimes in the dark night you can hear the rustle of wings. There is nothing to be seen, but you hear a cry, a dreadful laughter floating down from the heights. "Hokioi – Hokioi" is the cry, and as it ceases you hear that eerie whistle as a bird swoops down and up again into the blackness and silence of the night sky.

It is Hokioi, the unseen bird, calling his own name in triumph so that Kahu the hawk may hear and be ashamed. This is the story.

In the olden days Kahu and Hokioi quarrelled.

"You are large and clumsy," said Kahu, "and for all your size and strength you can only flutter about amongst the trees like Titi-pounamu the little rifleman."

"You are a boaster, an empty boaster," Hokioi screamed. "I can fly far higher than you. I could fly right out of your sight." He was nearly blind with rage. "Quickly, quickly," he screamed again, his eyes bright and hard as he looked at Kahu, "I challenge you. Let us begin at once and all the birds may see who is the clumsy one."

Kahu saw that all the birds had been listening so he accepted Hokioi's challenge. They flapped their wings and flew up into the sky. Hokioi kept looking up, straining his muscles to fly farther and faster than Kahu. The hawk flew with his eyes on the ground, as he always does, and presently he saw a cloud of smoke rolling up from the forest and red tongues of flame licking up above the trees. In a moment he had forgotten Hokioi's challenge and with a cry of joy he glided swiftly downwind to the edge of the forest to wait for the rats and lizards which would come scurrying away from the fire.

Hokioi knew nothing of this. His eyes were still fixed on the blue sky, and his tireless wings beat the air as he went up and up. He flew so far that the watching birds lost sight of him. Day changed to night and all the stars came out, and still Hokioi flew on. The morning rays flushed the sky before he stopped and looked down. There was no sign of Kahu and the very earth itself had disappeared.

That is why he has never been seen by mortal man; but on dark nights he flies low once more and mocks Kahu by calling out his own name:

"Hokioi – Hokioi!"

Popoia the Owl

In the days when Mataora rescued his wife from the torchlit land and took her up to the world of light, Tiwaiwaka the fantail was the chief of the birds of the Underworld. The path that Mataora and his wife travelled was long and dangerous, and Tiwaiwaka sent Popoia the owl and Peka the bat to bear them company and to show them the way.

Mataora had to fight his way out and he feared that his guides would be killed, so he hid them in the overhanging bush, in caves, and in every dark place that could not easily be seen. That is why Popoia and Peka love the darkness. They have become used to the gloom and cannot see clearly in the daytime.

When you see Popoia the owl blinking sleepily in the daylight you will know that he cannot see very well in the sunshine, and that perhaps he is thinking of the mice he will be eating when the friendly night comes round again. And you will remember how he and Peka helped Mataroa and Niwareka to reach the wind-blown spaces of the sunlit world.

Miromiro the Tomtit

The white-breasted tomtit is a cheery, bright-eyed little fellow, always on the watch for insects. "Ma te kanohi miromiro," says the Maori when he sees anyone looking for a lost article – "Oh for the eye of a tomtit."

Father Miromiro loves his wife and when she is busy building a nest for the brown-speckled eggs, he takes great care of her, bringing grass and twigs to help in the building and supplying her with food.

That is why he is sent to bring back runaway wives and husbands. Sometimes men and women get tired of their homes and run away. The cheeky little Miromiro is sent to bring them back. No matter how far they have gone, Miromiro flies after them. When he finds them he lights on their heads and straightaway they long for their homes once more.

Happy little Miromiro, the Messenger of Love!

What Kaka Stole from Kakariki

Once upon a time Kakariki, the beautiful parakeet, had a red breast. He was a handsome fellow with his crimson breast and green coat. The Kaka was jealous of that red breast. His plumage was dull and brown and he longed for the bright colours of Kakariki.

"Foolish bird," he said to Kakariki, "foolish one, you should hide your red breast."

Kakariki chattered indignantly. "Why should I hide my colours?" he asked. "Red, red as the blood of Kai-tangata, everyone admires them."

"Ah, little one," said Kaka gently, "how foolish you are. When Tane gave me my brown feathers, he gave me his best gift. Brown is the colour of our Mother Earth and the insects do not see me until my beak darts out and their lives are ended. Brown is the colour that Tane loves."

"But Tane has clothed Mother Earth in robes of green," said Kakariki, coming closer to Kaka, "and red is the sky at sunset. Surely Tane loves green and red the best."

"Not so, Kakariki. You may grieve, but he has not loved you, else he would not have given you those gaudy colours."

Kakariki looked in shame on his red breast and tried to cover it with his wings. "How can I lose my red feathers?" he asked sadly.

"There is only one way," said Kaka. "Give them to me. For love of you I will take the red feathers and hide them under my wings where none can see them."

Kakariki stripped off his red feathers and Kaka fastened them to his wings. With a hoarse cry of joy he spread them and sailed above the tree-tops. Into the glow of the setting sun he rose. Then Kakariki saw how beautiful Kaka had become and he knew that with his honeyed words Kaka had robbed him of his heritage. Kakariki's coat now is green but Kaka glows with his bright red feathers for all the world to see.

You can hear the song of Kakariki as he mourns for his feathers; but he chuckles too, as he chatters with his friends in the trees. Perhaps he thinks Tane cares more for him now that he is no longer red.

Kawau and the Tide Rips

When Kupe came to Aotearoa he brought Kereru the dove and Kawau the shag with him. Kereru was given the task of finding seeds and plants in the new land and Kawau was sent to explore the harbours for tidal and river currents.

On arrival at the Manukau Harbour, Kupe sent Kawau on ahead to explore every harbour from Manukau, where the Pakeha built the city of Auckland a thousand years later, to Te Whanganui-a-Tara where Wellington now stands. On his return he reported that the currents were not strong, so Kupe sailed for the southern harbour and pitched his camp there. After a while birds from the Canoe of Maui (the South Island) came to visit Kereru and Kawau.

"Where do you live?" asked Kereru.

"We come from the other island."

"What sort of food do you eat?"

"Many, many seeds that are good for the children of Tane."

Kawau thrust his head forward eagerly. "What are the currents like in your land?" he asked. "I have seen Raukawa (Cook Strait), but only in name is it great. Its currents are weak."

The birds of the south set up a deafening outcry.

"In our land the currents are strong. Come and see for yourself. We will guide you."

Kawau took wing and the other birds led him to the pass that lies between Rangitoto (D'Urville Island) and the mainland.

"Look!" they cried. Kawau saw below him the fierce tide rips and currents of the famous pass.

"Here is water worthy of a test," he cried and flew down.

It was not like the gentle heaving of the tide on the broad ocean, nor yet like the angry waves of the storm. Rather was it like water plunging down a precipice. One of Kawau's wings touched the water and was drawn below the surface as if a giant hand had plucked it down. He fell on his knees and stretched out the other wing in an attempt to span the pass, but the water seized him and hurled him down its steep slope, breaking his wing. So died the brave one of Kupe.

Kawau remains at the place where he fell, for there is a rock in French Pass which they say is Kawau, Kupe's bird. Had he overcome the water, the pass would have been blocked, but because his wing was broken, Maori and Pakeha may dare the strong currents and tide rips of Te Aumati, the pass between Rangitoto and the great southern island.

Why the Dotterel has a Brown Chest

Pihoihoi the ground-lark and Kukuruatu the dotterel were not always birds. Long ago they were two young men who were both in love with a beautiful girl whose name was Whano. They were not the first who had loved her, but every one of her suitors had been captured by Whano's grandmother and imprisoned.

"We must be careful," Pihoihoi said to his friend. "You go first and see if you can win her. If you do not return, I will know you have failed, and I will take my chance."

Kukuruatu was overjoyed by his friend's generosity. He crept silently towards the whare where Whano lived with her grandmother, but the old woman heard him coming. She seized him and thrust him into a strong building from which he was unable to escape. Then she branded him across his chest with hot charcoal to punish him for his presumption.

When Kukuruatu did not return, Pihoihoi knew he had a difficult task; but when he saw the girl afar off, he knew that the prize was worth the risk. He went up to the whare fearlessly. The old woman stretched out her hands to seize him, but he dodged lightly away.

"Wait a moment," he said, laughing, "Don't be in such a hurry to capture me. Listen first to the song I have to sing."

Standing well away from her, he lifted up his head and sang an unusual song which throbbed with love and laughter and brought Whano to the door to listen. As he finished the old woman reached out her clawed hands again, but once more Pihoihoi stepped lightly aside.

"Listen to the second verse of my song," he said. The lovely notes floated on the air. Pihoihoi sprang from side to side like a leaf in the wind. One of his fluttering movements took him to the door of the whare. In a flash he put his arms round the girl and carried her away.

"Come back! Come back!" the old woman shouted, but Pihoihoi was flying like a bird with his lovely burden. He changed in shape as he flew, until he became like the little singing bird we now know as Pihoihoi the lark.

What happened to Kukuruatu we cannot tell, except that he also became a bird which bears on its breast the dark mark placed there by the grandmother of Whano.

Kawau the Shag

Uta spent the day fishing. Towards evening he beached his canoe and waited for his wife to come and take the fish to the storehouse. He waited until the sun had set and the stars came out, and went up the track through the bracken to his house to see what had happened to her.

"Why have you not come to bring the fish?" he demanded. "That is woman's work."

"Your children have been naughty, and I had to look after them. I will go now."

She disappeared in the darkness. Uta did not know that Houmea, his wife, was really an ogress. He would have been amazed if he had seen her then. She threw the fish into her mouth, eating them raw without removing the scales. By the time her hunger was satisfied, the fish had all gone. Houmea dragged her feet through the sand and broke branches off the bushes, scattering the leaves. She called to her husband that the fish had been stolen. Uta rushed down to the beach.

"No one can have been here," he cried.

"They must have. Look at their footprints, and see where they have come through the bushes!"

With that Uta had to be satisfied.

The following day he went fishing again, but his suspicions had been aroused. When he returned, he told his children to hide in the bushes to see what would happen. Then he went up to the house and sent his wife to bring the fish. Once again she ate them whole and raw, but this time the children were watching, and they reported what had happened to their father. That night there was a fierce quarrel between Uta and Houmea. The man realised that he had married an evil ogress ... but food had still to be procured. The following day he set out in his canoe. As soon as he was out of sight Houmea turned on her children and swallowed them at a single gulp.

That night Uta waited by the shore in vain. He could not see his children anywhere, but his wife was waiting for him in the whare.

"Where are my children?" he asked.

"They have gone away for a while," she answered sullenly.

Uta did not believe her. He suspected what had happened, and repeated an incantation. His wife opened her mouth involuntarily until it gaped like the entrance to a cavern. Suddenly the children tumbled out. Uta asked them to fetch the fish from the canoe. When they put their load down in front of him, he scaled the fish and put them in the oven which he had lit in readiness. When they were cooked, Houmea came out of the whare.

"Open your mouth," he ordered. He took a hot stone from the bottom of the oven and threw it into her mouth. The ogress turned black and fell in pieces in front of him – but she lives on in Kawau the shag who, like Houmea, has an ever-greedy throat.

So died Kawau,
the brave one of Kupe.

Tiwaiwaka the Fantail

Tiwaiwaka fluttered restlessly round the whare of the fire goddess, Mahuika. The walls were charred by fire, and the green bush had been burnt to the ground. Smoke was still rising from the desolate land which had been destroyed by flames.

Of Mahuika herself there was no sign. The half-god Maui had stolen the seeds of fire, and when Mahuika found out what he had done, she tried to destroy him. Now Maui had come back to try to find her. He searched everywhere in vain. Then he saw Tiwaiwaka the fantail, and before she could flutter out of his reach, he grasped her firmly in his hand and tried to make her tell him where his ancestor had gone.

"No," she said, "I will not tell you."

Maui squeezed the bird's head until her eyes nearly popped out, and her tail spread and struck out at an angle from her body.

"Tell me!" Maui said fiercely. "Tell me where she has gone."

Tiwaiwaka could stand the pain no longer.

"I don't know," she said. "I don't know where she has gone."

"Then tell me where she has hidden the fire. I know that she has hidden it, and I want to take it back to my people."

"If it is a gift for men," Tiwaiwaka replied, "I will tell you where it is. When you get back to your own home, take two pieces of the kaikomako tree and rub them together. That is where Mahuika has hidden the fire. It is there, inside the kaikomako tree. When you rub two pieces of the wood of that tree together, you will find that the fire is there, waiting to come out and do your bidding."

Little Tiwaiwaka's eyes are still prominent in her head, and her tail sticks out at an angle because Maui held her so roughly when he was searching for the seeds of fire. But Tiwaiwaka does not care. The broad fan of her tail is like the sail of a ship, and she is able to twist and turn in the air as she snaps up the insects on which she feeds.

Tautoru the Bird-hunter

Of all the bird-hunters of old, the most renowned was Tautoru. He was young and handsome and skilled in all the arts of hunting. The snares which he made and decorated with bright berries and scented flowers attracted flocks of birds from a great distance. The plump wood-pigeons alighted, unaware of the cunningly concealed nooses that were hidden beneath the foliage, and there they met their death. To the snare came kakas and tuis, and birds which were seldom seen and never caught, even the elusive kotuku and the kakakura. It is said that as many birds were caught in a single day as twenty young men could carry. Kiwis, wekas, and kakapos, the ground birds of the forest, were not safe from him, because he trained dogs to hunt them.

Tautoru did not depend wholly on his skill, but was also constant in the rituals and karakias recited to Tane, the lord of the forest. He was admired by his fellow-tribesmen, and even won the love of Rauroha, who was the foremost of the spirits of the air. She descended each night and stayed with him till dawn, sharing his love, but ever hiding her face from him. Tautoru longed to see the woman he loved and, by violating the tapu that surrounded her, he succeeded in looking at her in the first light of dawn.

But alas, Rauroha could no longer live with him. Knowing that he had lost her for ever, Tautoru went sorrowfully into the forest. He climbed a tall tree and set his snare in the branches, but he had no heart for his task. Placing his foot carelessly, he slipped and fell to the ground, breaking his neck.

There was no one to see him except his lost wife. Looking down from the heavens, she was puzzled to see a countless host of birds wheeling and crying round one of the forest trees. She descended and found her husband lying quiet in death at the foot of the tree. She wept over him, and sent a message to his relatives to tell them of the young man's death. They carried him home on a stretcher in a sitting position, clad in his finest robes.

On the journey a mysterious thing happened. Suddenly the bearers found that their load was lightened, for Tautoru's body disappeared. When they returned home with the empty stretcher, the tohungas explained that Tane, the first bird-snarer, must have taken him up to the sky because of his great exploits on earth. He has remained there ever since as a constellation of stars. The Pakeha calls it Orion, but to the Maori it is Tautoru, who forever spears pigeons in the star-spangled skies. The cluster of flowers and the snare itself are traced in the constellation; and, if one looks closely, myriads of tiny pigeons can be seen winging towards the snare.

24

Stories of
Insects and Lizards

The Ant and the Cicada

In the summer the New Zealand forest quivers with the song of Kikihi the cicada. The air trembles with sound, the sun shines through the leaves as the warm wind gently stirs the foliage, and winter seems far away. That is the burden of the song of Kikihi. "The winter is past and summer is here. Let us sing our song on the warm bark of the trees and be glad, for cold and darkness have gone away for ever."

But there is another song that few have heard, because they are deafened by Kikihi. It is a little song, sung by those who are working through the summer days, near the ground, close to the warm earth. It is the song of Popokorua the ant. "Winter is coming," he sings, as he scurries round, collecting food and storing it away. "We need food to keep us alive in the cold days of winter. Let us work to live."

The days pass and winter comes. The leaves that danced in the sunshine shiver in the cold wind and icy rain flows over them down to the sodden earth.

Then Kikihi, who was warm and happy and carefree in the summer time, grows thin and cold and in the end he dies, clinging to the unfriendly bark. But Popokorua is warm and snug in his home, well-fed, and looking forward once more to the coming of summer.

The Mosquito and the Sandfly

In their home by a dark pool in the forest, shaded from the sun by giant trees and the raupo that fringed it, Naeroa the mosquito and Namu the sandfly met one day.

Kikihi basked in the sun
while the ants were hard at work.

"What deed of bravery can we do?" asked Namu.

Naeroa beat his gauzy wings till they whined in the still air.

"There is a deed that we can do that will bring fame to us. Let us attack man!"

Namu danced in the air in his excitement. "Yes," he cried, "let us go now. Let us taste the blood of man!"

Naeroa the mosquito shook his head. "You are too impatient, friend Namu. If we attack him now he will see us coming and we will be defeated. Wait until night-time. Man cannot see at night. Then is the time to plunge in and draw his blood."

But Namu was impatient to be gone. "I shall not wait. I am not afraid of man," he boasted. "You may wait for the cloak of night to be drawn across the sky. My people will attack in the light of the sun. Many will be killed, but we shall defeat him."

With that he called softly and his brothers rose up like a black cloud and flew above the trees. Naeroa settled down on a leaf and watched them go.

The pool drowsed in the sunshine, for the sunbeams had broken through the overhanding trees, and Naeroa slept undisturbed.

When the sun had gone and the pool grew blacker in the shadow of the trees, he looked up. Namu the sandfly was circling round the pool. He flew lower and settled close to Naeroa.

"How did the battle go?" asked Naeroa with a gleam in his eye.

In reply Namu sank his head and sang the song of defeat. "We tasted blood," he said when the song was ended. "He could not stop us. But man is very strong. Slap! went his great hand, and my brothers have died in thousands. Slap! went his hand again when we settled, and only I have returned. My brothers are dead."

"You did wrong to go in the daylight," Naeroa said. "I warned you."

Namu lifted his head proudly. "We were defeated," he said," but we are not beaten. Man is our enemy. We shall attack again and again. We shall never give in."

"Ah, but you have been defeated now," Naeroa said. "My way is best."

He sprang lightly into the air, and as he winged his way up in the faint starlight the mosquito people followed, flying silently in the darkness.

Man did not know of their coming. He lay down in his whare and closed his eyes. But presently he moved. A shrill whining filled the air. It came closer. It was a sound to chill the blood.

Suddenly the whining stopped. "Ah ha," said Man. 'it is Naeroa. He has settled on me, but as I killed Namu and his people, so I will destroy Naeroa." He slapped his arm, but Naeroa was not there. Close to his ear came the shrill song of battle. Man struck himself till his head rang with the blow, but Naeroa had settled on his leg and was drinking his blood.

He felt the sting of it and sat up to strike the place, but Naeroa was gone and one of his people was gliding down to Man's shoulder.

For hour after hour Man fought with Naeroa. Naeroa's silence was as terrifying as his high-pitched whine. When morning came, Naeroa flew away with his warriors, leaving Man battered and swollen and blood-stained.

Namu heard him coming, singing the song of victory, and he was glad because his defeat had been avenged.

So it was the Namu and Naeroa are the enemies of Man, and so it is that they still attack him, Namu by day and Naeroa by night. But Naeroa is he that is dreaded by Man!

The Dog and the Lizard

The taniwha Kaiwhakaruaki was dead, and from its tail had come the lizards.* Everywhere one looked there were lizards, brown and green and grey, lying motionless on hot rocks in the sunshine, or scuttling under stones and loose bark on trees. There were many dogs too, black dogs and white dogs with long bodies, thick tails and pointed jaws. They had no love for each other, the dogs and lizards of Maoriland.

And so when Lizard and Dog met each other one day on a narrow path fringed with taramoa, the clinging bush-lawyer, one would not give way to the other.

"The forest paths belong to me," Dog said loudly and arrogantly. Lizard stood staunchly on the bare ground, bracing his legs and refusing to be intimidated by Dog. Seeing that neither would retire and let the other past, they both went back and reported the

---

* See page 181.

matter to their tribes. There was fierce argument in the assembly of the dog tribe, and also of the lizards, but on one thing they were both agreed, that this was a cause for war.

The tribes gathered together and met in an open space. They fought fiercely, but the lizards were no match for the strong teeth of the dogs, and they were badly defeated.

When the battle was over, the dogs were surfeited with lizard flesh; but it is said that this huge meal of lizards affected the fertility of the dogs for ever after; and perhaps it is true, for the Maori dog is as dead as the moa.

The Shark and the Lizard

Such a harmless, inoffensive creature is the lizard that we may wonder at its temerity in defying the dog tribe. Yet the lizard was an object of fear to the Maori; perhaps because it was akin to the vast taniwhas of rivers, lakes, and dark chasms.

And were not the lizard and the shark children of one father? In the beginning of time they both lived in the sea. Lizard was the elder brother. After the battle between Tawhiri-matea the god of wind and Tangaroa the god of ocean, Lizard grew disgusted with is brother Shark, and left the sea. He crawled up the beach and climbed on to a rock where he could feel the warm sunshine on his back.

Shark swam as close to him as he could and called, "Why don't you stay in the water with me?"

Lizard replied, "I am happy here in the sunshine and the cooling breeze. What advantage would there be in staying with you in the restless waters and dark places of the ocean?"

"There is freedom here. We do not have to shelter in holes in the rocks, nor hide from the claws and sharp beaks of the birds."

"The deep water would be equally dangerous for me, brother."

Shark opened his eyes wide in surprise. "But the water is our home. How could it possibly be dangerous?"

Lizard had grown tired of the conversation. He felt that the only way to stop his persistent brother was to insult him. He was silent, trying to think of a curse that would mortally offend him. Ah! Let me compare him with cooked food; then he will be angry and go away!

"Dangerous? Of course it is dangerous. If I stayed with you I might be caught by the fish-hooks of Man, and taken away for food – and that is what is going to happen to you some day. You will become a tasty morsel in the food basket, you see!"

Shark lashed his tail in fury and snapped vainly with his murderous jaws.

"Stay where you are, then," he shouted. "One day there will be a fire in the fern and you will be roasted. See how you like that!"

Lizard tossed its head and laughed. "You don't know me. I will glare with my wide open eyes and cry 'Peu!' They will think I am the father of demons as I stand with my spines erect. Man will look at me with fear and I shall rule the land."

He wagged his long tail, turned round and slid down the rock, disappearing in the grass and bracken, ready to begin to terrify the sons of Tu.

25

Stories of Giants, Flying Men and Walking Mountains

The Flying Taniwha

A curious grey mass lay on the beach at Patea, looking like a rock in the dusk. A hunter hurrying home to his kainga saw the unusual sight and went across the sand to see what it might be. The waves washed round it and scooped the sand from its sides as they ran back down the slope of the beach. When the hunter touched it with his spear it yielded like flesh so, believing it to be some strange fish, he plunged his weapon into its body. The sleeping monster roared with pain and hurled itself at its tormentor. A horny claw shot out and grasped him round the waist. Two wings like the sails of a canoe unfolded themselves and flapped in the air. The hunter was picked up from the beach and borne aloft, for the strange monster was a flying taniwha.

The hunter looked at the sand streaming past just beneath him. Overhead the wings were beating strongly, rising higher into the air. As the moon rose it grew colder. Forest and lake spread themselves out far below like another world. Presently they left the land behind them, and nothing could be seen but tiny white-capped waves shining in the moonlight, and filmy wisps of cloud that clung for a moment and were lost behind them.

All night long they flew, and when morning came the sun rose on another land. It was Hawaiki, the homeland of the Maori people. The taniwha circled round and landed in a clearing surrounded by tall trees. The hunter had no eyes for the lovely tropical flowers and fruit that hung on the trees and rioted over the ground. Everywhere he looked were taniwha, huge creatures with unblinking eyes, folded wings and strong bird-like claws.

The taniwha that had captured him began to speak in a voice

that sounded like the rumbling of an avalanche, but the hunter could understand most of the words.

"This common fellow wounded me. He must die the death."

"Where does he come from?" asked an older taniwha.

"From Kupe's land. He is a man who lives on the Fish of Maui."

"What were you doing there, O taniwha?"

"I was resting."

"Where were you resting, O taniwha?"

"On the beach at Patea."

"Were you on the sand or in the water?"

"As I lay asleep on the beach the water caught me unawares."

An old taniwha, bleached white with the passing of a thousand years, heaved himself to his feet and stretched his tattered wings.

"O taniwha," he said in his deep voice, "your own tongue has judged you. The air is your home; the land for you and us when we are tired. The air is not the place for water-taniwha; the water is no place for taniwha of the air. This man did right to try and kill you in the place where you were found."

The circle of taniwha nodded in agreement.

"What shall we do with the man?" asked one of the younger ones.

The oldest taniwha pointed a horny talon at him. "You shall bear him back to the Fish of Maui, youngest of taniwha," he said. "Take him now."

So the hunter was taken home. As they drew near to Patea he reached up and plucked a few feathers from the taniwha's wings. These feathers became a precious possession. One of them he gave to Tama-ahua of Whanganui. Tama had another home at Waitotara, but the journey there was long and tiring. With one of the taniwha's feathers he became a sort of taniwha himself, and in the cold moonlight he would float above the tree-tops from Whanganui to Waitotara with the magic talisman clasped in his hand.

Matau the Giant of Wakatipu

In the high country of Murihiku lived Manata, daughter of an ariki, and her lover Matakauri. Manata's father would not let the lovers marry. He planned to give his daughter to a powerful chief who lived on the Taieri Plains.

One morning Manata was missing. No trace of her could be found and she had taken nothing with her, for her sleeping mats and cloak lay where they had been tossed when she left. It was a mystery until one of the searchers found the print of a huge foot in the soft clay by the river, and another remembered that the earth had shaken in the night.

"It is Matau who has taken her away," the chief said when they brought these reports to him.

The people drew closer together when they heard the dreaded name, for Matau was a giant who lived among the snow-capped mountains of the hinterland, and was feared through all Otakou.

"I will give Manata in marriage to any man who will rescue her," the chief said in his grief.

No one stirred except Matakauri. In the silence he hurried to the door and began to climb up the mountain steps to Matau's lair. In the broad daylight he came upon Manata sitting beneath a flax bush by the river. When she saw him coming she ran to him and hid her face on his shoulder.

"Go back, my beloved," she said. "I cannot escape. You will be killed if the giant awakes."

Matakauri smiled. "While the warm north-west wind blows, Matau will sleep. It is only when the wind changes that he will awake."

"But you do not know what has happened. See, he has tied me to his waist with this cord."

Matakauri laughed as he raised his axe and struck the cord, but the axe bounced off it, for it was made from the hide of the two-headed dog which cannot be cut by greenstone.

Manata's tears rolled down her face. One of them fell on the thong and as if by magic, it parted. Smiling through her tears, Manata helped her lover to make a raft of manuka, tied with tough vines and interlaced with korari to give it buoyancy. They sprang aboard and were soon back at their home, where Manata's father greeted them as though they had risen from the dead.

"I have not finished my work," Matakauri said. "The north-west wind still blows, but the time will come when the giant will wake up. We shall never be safe then, but now he is asleep and a man may take him unawares."

Matakauri set fire to the bracken
round the sleeping giant.

No one offered to go with Matakauri as he climbed the hills for the second time. He passed the flax bush where he had found Manata and followed the dogskin cord which lay along the river flat and up the hill that casts its shadow over the valley. The giant lay across the mountains with his head pillowed on one mountain peak and his feet on another. Miles away towards the setting sun Matakauri worked day after day while the warm wind blew, piling bracken and dried grass round the sleeping giant.

When his work was finished he kindled a flame with his fire-stick and set the bracken alight. The mountain tops burst into flame and a cloud of smoke veiled the bright sunshine.

The giant was consumed in the flames. They blazed so fiercely that the earth itself was set alight. A thousand feet deep was the hole they made, following the form of the sleeping giant. Then came the rain and the mountain streams poured their waters into the streaming hole and filled it to the brim, where the giant lies sleeping quietly through the centuries.

Wakatipu men call it, this lake of the cold south. Deep beneath its surface Matau's heart lies beating. It was only the heart of the giant that resisted the flames, and as it beats the lake waters gently rise and fall.

The Giant and the Whale

There is a mark on a rock at East Cape which is just like the print of a giant human foot. Eighty miles to the south, not far from the present town of Gisborne, there is a creek, and in one of its banks is the fossil skeleton of a whale. At Tokomaru Bay, which is half way between East Cape and Gisborne, there are three hills quite close to each other, like the corners of a triangle.

Once upon a time there was a giant who lived in the South Island. One day he paid a visit to the North Island. When he came to the waters that divided the two islands, he took a stride that carried him from one to the other. In the strait of Raukawa a whale was lying on the water. The giant saw the puff of steamy vapour floating on the breeze, and in a flash he stretched out his hand and picked up the whale. Tucking it under his arm he went along the coast until he reached the bank of a little river. There he sat down and ate the whale, skin and all, leaving only the bony skeleton which was too hard for his teeth. Then he stretched himself out on the soft mattress of the trees and slept.

The Maoris who lived in that place were not pleased to see the giant. One of his feet had flattened all their young kumara plants, and even now his arm blocked the entrance to their pa. While his breath swayed the tree-tops they prepared a trap for him at Tokomaru. It was made with a tall tree which was stripped of all its branches and fastened to the ground with rope. They hoped the giant would put his foot in it and be caught.

He woke up, and when he had taken a few paces he saw the trap. As he passed he kicked it contemptuously. The released spring crashed into a hill and split it into three separate peaks. Another step carried him on to the East Cape, where he dived into the sea and was never seen again.

Is the story true? Who knows? But on the East Cape is the mark of a giant's foot. At a creek near Gisborne is the fossil skeleton of a whale. At Tokomaru Bay there are three small peaks, close together like the corners of a triangle.

Restless Mountains

In the days of the gods, many mountains lived happily together at Taupo in the middle of the Fish of Maui. They ate and worked and played and loved together, but with the passing of time quarrels arose between them. Some of the younger ones travelled north and south, striding swiftly through the night until they were stopped by the rising sun.

Tongariro, Ruapehu and Ngauruhoe were the only ones who remained. Tongariro took to wife Pihanga, a dainty little mountain who lived nearby. Their children were Snow, Hail, Rain and Sleet.

Pihanga loved the white-headed Tongariro, and when broad-shouldered Taranaki tried to win her affections, her husband rose in his anger and drove Taranaki to the west. As he rushed to the sea he left behind him the narrow deep-cut channel of the Whanganui River. When he reached the sea he felt safe from Tongariro's vengeance, although he could still see the wind-blown smoke pouring from the summit of the angry mountain.

Taranaki shrugged his shoulders and wandered slowly up the coast. He rested for a while at Ngaere, and when he moved on again a great depression was left in the ground, which afterwards became the Ngaere swamp.

As daylight broke, Taranaki reached the end of the land, and there he will remain forever. Sometimes he is veiled in mist, for then he is weeping for Pihanga. And sometimes Tongariro remembers the impudence of distant Taranaki and the flames of anger leap in his breast until a dense cloud of black smoke hangs over his head.

And what of the young ones who fled northward? Putauaki (Mount Edgecombe) had two wives who went with him. One of them was Pohaturoa, the castle-like rock on the Waikato River at Atiamuri. She took so long to cook a meal that Putauaki was caught by the swiftly advancing daylight. Some of their children scattered and became islands in the Bay of Plenty, and rocks in the Whakatane River. Whakaari (White Island) and Moutohora (Whale Island) were two others who were petrified by the rising sun. Ruawahia accompanied them part of the way, but he met Mahoihoi, a famous tohunga, and quarrelled with him. Ruawahia struck the priest, who warded off the blow, and gave another in return which split the mountain where it stood.

Maungapohatu and his wife Kakaramea, who is called Rainbow Mountain by the Pakeha, also lived by the shore of Lake Taupo. Maungapohatu wanted to go northwards with the other mountains, but Kakaramea insisted on travelling southwards. They argued for some time, until at length Maungapohatu went north with his children, leaving his wife behind. Kakaramea remained grieving by the lakeside, until she could no longer bear to be without her children. She left her home and followed swiftly after them, but the sun stopped her at Waiotapu, south of Rotorua, where she stands, lonely in her beautiful garments of glowing colours, severed from her husband and children until there comes another night of magic when the sundered mountains may be joined together again.

Kakepuku is a lonely mountain on the borders of the King Country. He travelled up from the south until he came to the banks of the Waipa River. There he saw a beautiful girl mountain whose name was Kawa. She was the daughter of Pirongia and Taupiri. As soon as he saw the lovely shape of the little mountain, Kakepuku fell in love with her, and remained by her side. But there were two other mountains who loved the same fair, rounded hill ... Karewa, a bold, rocky peak, and Puke-tarata, a fern-clad mountain range on the far side of the swamps. They were jealous of the favours Kawa showed to Kakepuku and fought fiercely with him. Puke-tarata was soon injured and retied to nurse his wounds, but Karewa continued the struggle. Both mountains called volcanic fires to their aid. Dense plumes of choking smoke rolled from their summits, and shimmering white lava trickled down their sides as they struggled in a fiery embrace. Thunder echoed from peak to peak, and the dark smoke clouds were lit by bright flashes of lightning. Trees were burned and rivulets dried up, and the ground shook beneath their stamping feet.

Presently Karewa weakened and fled before Kakepuku, vainly trying to ward off the white-hot rocks that were hurled at him. All the long night he blundered through swamp and fern, and through the western ocean, until daylight halted his progress, and he became fixed and immovable far from the coast and the little mountain he had loved so dearly.* Long soft clouds sometimes stream from his summit, wafted on the wind, and light on Kawa to remind her that he cherishes her still.

As for Kawa, she loves the mighty Kakepuku. With her back turned to timid Puke-tarata, she stretches her arms toward her loved one across the valley. When the fog unites the male and female mountains in its gentle embrace, the Maori says, "This is indeed a night for the marriage of Kakepuku and Kawa."

In the grey dim days in the beginning of time the South Island was visited by a half-legendary canoe named Arai-te-uru. Many are the tales that are told of her and her crew as she sailed along the eastern coast, and was wrecked near Moeraki. You can see the petrified canoe in the rocks, with her captain standing proudly amidships, and the curious round boulders which, they say, are the calabashes that were washed ashore when she struck the rocks.

---

* Karewa is called Gannet Island on present-day maps.

Amongst those who escaped were a boy named Kirikiri-katata and a girl named Aroaro-kaehe. Amongst their friends was a small boy whose name was Aoraki. As the shipwrecked sailors travelled overland, the boy's legs grew tired and one of the men carried him on his shoulders. Presently they came in sight of majestic Mount Cook, the tallest of all the mighty mountains of the Southern Alps.

"What shall we call this great mountain?" someone asked.

"It must have a good name because it is the highest peak we have seen," said another. "Let us name it after the tallest person who is here."

The others agreed. They looked round and found that little Aoraki was the tallest of them all as he rode on the shoulders of his big friend.

"Aoraki!" they shouted. "Let that be the name," and they smiled at the thought, because Aoraki means Cloud in the Sky.*

And so the mountain was given the name we are proud to remember. But there is another name, too, for the flanks of this greatest of mountains. Tahatane, the man's side, was called Kirikiri-katata, and tahawahine, the woman's side, was called Aroaro-kaehe – and these, you will remember, were the names of Aoraki's friends.

In those far-off days it is said that men and women could stride from peak to peak like giants, and even change themselves into vast pyramids of rock and move about the land.

The father of Kirikiri and Aroaro became a mountain. He was big and strong, and was changed into the hill we know as Mount Peel, while his wife became Little Mount Peel. Whether Kirikiri and Aroaro were changed into mountains we do not know. There are some who say that they were turned into trees on the slopes of Mount Peel and that these two, brother and sister, married and had four children. They were tiny hills which moved away from their parents and settled down as four small mountains. They stayed there through the long, long years until the white man came to Canterbury and called them the Four Peaks.

---

* If there is any truth in the legend it is probable that Aoraki was himself named after a mountain peak in Tahiti.

26

Stories of
Plants and Trees

The Kumara

Of all the foods which were known to the Maori, there was none so highly regarded as the kumara or sweet potato. It was not like fernroot or puwha or berries which could be gathered as they grew on the plains or in the forest. The tubers had to be planted in carefully prepared soil and kept weeded and free of caterpillars. There were ceremonies and rites to be observed if the kumara god were to watch over his crop and care for it.

When they came to Aotearoa, the Maoris brought some of the prized tubers with them – or else they came in some miraculous fashion, as we have heard in the story of Pou and his great bird.

Once upon a time the kumara was not be found anywhere on earth. It lived in the sky under the protection of the star Whanui. In those days there was a married couple, Rongo-maui and Pani, who lived in the land of Mataora. They heard that the wonderful food could be found in the far-off places of the sky. Rongo left his wife and climbed up to heaven where he found the star-god in his home. He asked him to give him some of his treasured children, the kumara tubers, but Whanui refused.

"They are mine," he said, "and they will remain with me for ever in my home."

Rongo-maui went to the corner of the whare. He lay down on a sleeping mat and pretended he was overcome by fatigue after his long journey. He closed his eyes and began to snore. Whanui kept awake for a time but presently his head began to nod.

Rongo opened his eyes and looked at Whanui who was sitting with his back to the wall and his chin on his breast. He sat up slowly, but Whanui did not move. He stood up and tiptoed across

Rongo stole the kumaras
of the sleeping god.

to the star-god, but still Whanui did not stir. Inch by inch his hand crept across to the basket by the god and his fingers gathered up a few tubers. He moved quietly down the whare, slipped out of the door and closed it softly behind him. In frenzied haste lest Whanui should waken and discover that some of his kumaras had been taken, he scrambled back to earth.

It was the first time that anything had ever been stolen in land or sea or sky, but it was a theft which was of great benefit to mankind. Whanui does not forget his children who have come down to earth. When he first appears as a twinkling speck of light in the eastern sky, the wise men of the tribe know that the time for planting the kumara has come, and that the star will smile on them when they make the holes to receive the tubers. Rongo-maui has become the father of the kumara and Pani is its mother.

There have been other kumara plantations in the sky. One of them was kept by the god Maru who was a relative of Maui, whom he had invited to stay with him before he returned to his mother and brothers. Maui grew from childhood to young manhood in the country of the sky, and learned many arts which were useful to him in later life. He saw that Maru had a fine crop of kumaras, so he cleared another patch of ground and planted a crop for himself. One day he went to see how Maru's kumaras were faring, and discovered that the plants were bigger and more healthy than his own. He was jealous of his relative's success and used his magic powers to create a heavy fall of snow. The snow and the bitter winds which followed shrivelled the leaves of Maru's plants while Maui's remained healthy. Maru saw what had happened and worked hard to save his crop, but only a few survived in a sheltered corner of the plantation.

He knew very well that the evil had come from Maui. Summoning the caterpillar tribe, he set them to work. They went in their thousands and ate every plant in Maui's plantation, leaving him without a single kumara. It was a feast which gave them an appetite for the leaves of the plant, and Maori workers must always be vigilant in picking them from the leaves lest the plants suffer the same fate as those in Maui's garden.

The Kauri and the Whale

The greatest of all ocean-dwellers, except the fabulous monster which swallows the seas, causing whirlpools which destroy canoes and men, is Tohora the whale. On land the mightiest living thing is the kauri, the giant tree of the northern lands, which stands straight and strong, waving its great branches in the wind.

If you look at the trunk of a kauri you will see that it has a smooth grey bark, and that it is full of an amber resin which is called kauri gum. Many years ago men used to search for this gum in the forks of the branches, and to dig for the fossil gum which lay in the ground, marking the place where kauri trees had flourished and died thousands of years before.

It was fitting that the giant of the forest and the giant of the sea should become friends. Tohora swam close to shore in the deep water below a forest-clad headland and called to his friend Kauri to come with him to the ocean.

"Come with me," he called. "If you stay here, men will cut you down to make a canoe. It is not safe for you to remain where you are."

Kauri shook his leafy arms. "Who am I to care for such funny little men," he said proudly. "They can do me no harm."

"Ah," said Tohora, 'you do not know. They may be small and insignificant, but their sharp greenstone axes will bite into you and their fire will burn you. Come with me while there is still time."

"No, Tohora," Kauri replied. "If I were to invite you to live here with me, you would lie helpless on the ground. Your weight would keep you pressed to the earth and you would not move as you do in the oceans. And if I were to follow you I would be tossed about by the storms, I would float helplessly on the water. My leaves would drop off and in the end I would sink down to the silent home of Tangaroa. I would no longer see the bright sun, and feel the soft rain on my leaves, and no longer would I stand up to fight the wind while my roots held me strong and firm on Mother Earth.

Tohora thought for a while. "What you say is true," he said at length, "yet you are my friend. I want to help you. I want you to remember me. Let us change our skins, in order that we may remember each other.

To this Kauri agreed. He gave his bark to Tohora and clothed himself in the skin of the whale which is smooth and grey; and the giant tree is as full of resin as its friend the whale is full of oil.

The Wandering Trees of the Plain

There were once two cabbage trees which bore the long name Ti-whakaaweawe-a-Ngatoro-i-rangi. Too long a name you might think for two wind-blown cabbage trees on the lonely Kaingaroa Plain. But listen first to the ancient tale.

Many hundreds of years before the white man came and planted exotic pines on the bare tableland, the famous tohunga of the Arawa canoe, Ngatoro-i-rangi, travelled across it with his sisters. They came from Hawaiki. They were weird women who held in their hands powers of fire and darkness and magic. Their names were Kuiwai and Haungaroa. They were followed by their women servants who carried food, but they had no need to take water with them, for when they were thirsty, Ngatoro stamped with his foot and springs of clear water bubbled through the soil. Halfway across the plain they stopped for a meal. Haungaroa was hungry after plodding for so many miles across the dusty pumice land, and she continued to eat long after her brother and sister had finished. The women who had carried the food laughed at her and whispered together, "What a long time Haungaroa is taking over her meal." From that day the plan was known as Te Kaingaroa-a-Haungaroa – the long meal of Haungaroa.

It was no laughing matter to the fierce woman tohunga. She was angry with her slaves and turned on them with biting words and heavy blows, driving them before her like the wind. Fear carried them beyond her reach, but she called down a worse fate and changed them into cabbage trees.

There are no other ti or cabbage trees like them in all the breadth and length of Aotearoa. They did not fasten their roots into the earth but were condemned to wander homeless and lost for ever on the plain where Haungaroa had taken so long to finish her meal. The Maoris called them Ti-whakaaweawe, the wandering cabbage trees of Ngatoro-i-rangi. Travellers would see them from afar, but they retreated before them only to appear suddenly in the mists that swirled across the pumice lands, and to follow them in the distance.

At length, grown old and tired, they rooted themselves and grew into tall, big-boled trees, and met their deaths, one at the greenstone adze of a Maori chief and the other at the steel blade of Pakeha's axe. The joke they had shared so briefly at Haungaroa's expense was over and peace had come at last.

The Hinau of Ruatahuna

The women of Tuhoe who wanted babies resorted to a tree that had been made fruitful by one of their ancestors. It was a venerable tree known as Te Iho-o-Kataka, and it had flourished for many years on a forest-clad ridge. A visitor whose name was Kataka had raised his hand to pluck some berries from this hinau tree when he heard a voice which said, "Do not eat my berries. I am the life-spirit of your child."

Kataka obeyed the voice which told him that the tree was sacred to his children.

The centuries passed slowly by, and still the hinau tree stood on the ridge, and many stories were told of its power.

Childless wives whispered to each other that the way to be sure of achieving motherhood was to go to the Iho of Kataka and to clasp the trunk of the tree in their arms.

Secretly they went there in the early morning or in the dusky evenings, accompanied by their husbands and a tohunga who showed them what to do. The side on which the rising sun shone was the male side, and where it sets was the female. So the young mother who wants a man child clasps the tree on its eastern side, while the one who needs a daughter (for there were a few women who, strangely enough in the eyes of their friends, preferred a girl to be born to them) went to the western side of the tree which brought new life to the world in their bodies.

The Singing Pohutukawa

Of other trees we could tell – of the pohutukawa that guards the entrance to the underworld at Cape Te Reinga, of the wishing tree of Hine-hopu, or of the manuka at Whakatane which was said to be the most sacred object in the land.

But let us end our stories with the tale of Tapuae the wind-omen tree of Ohoukaka Bay in Rotoiti. It hangs, gnarled and ancient, still gaily flaunting its scarlet blooms in summer, over the edge of a tall cliff. When the branches murmured drowsily like Ngaro the blowfly, it was a sign that there would be fair weather and blue skies, but if it whispered in the soft breezes, it was a warning of rain and wind. Sometimes the whisper song rose to a shrill screaming, and fishermen on the lake would paddle quickly when they heard it because they knew that a storm was coming.

There is magic in the trees, strong magic in all the children of Tane since the god of nature claimed them for this children, nurturing them with water and the dark soil of Mother Earth, and peopling them with his other, best-loved creation, the birds.

27

Stories of Greenstone

Whaiapu and Poutini

Hine-tu-a-hoanga, the guardian of the sandstone known as Whai-apu, was jealous of Ngahue and his prize greenstone which was called Poutini. If only he were somewhere else, or if only he did not own such a splendid, shining piece of jade, she would have been contented. She made sly remarks about him and told falsehoods which caused his friends to look at him out of the corners of their eyes. Ngahue's life became unbearable, and eventually he decided that there would be no peace for him unless he left his home at Hawaiki.

He prepared his canoe for a long sea voyage, and taking Poutini with him, he set sail not knowing where he was going save that he would be free of Hine's persecution. No sooner had he departed than Hine, whose heart should have been light, began to grieve for the loss of Ngahue's jade. Whaiapu and Poutini were ever at war, but they needed each other, for one was the grinding stone and the other the stone that was ground.

Hine had her canoe made ready in haste and followed her old enemy, keeping the top of his sail in sight above the horizon. Day after day she followed, until at length Ngahue landed on the island of Tuhua. Hine followed him ashore, but once again she found that she could not tolerate him for long, nor could Whaiapu and Poutini ever rest together in peace. Ngahue set sail again with Poutini, and the implacable Hine-tu-a-hoanga, perpetually linked to him by envy and malice, followed until they reached the shores of Aotearoa, which none had ever seen before.

Here was a land of misty, snow-clad mountains, of green forests and singing birds, and room for Ngahue to enjoy Poutini without interference. He was determined that the strife between the stones should cease, and did not rest until he came to the Arahura River, where he made an everlasting resting place for it. He buried it in the swift-running water where the trees murmured over it and the cold water lapped round it and foamed over its body.

Then he departed for his homeland; but with him went a tiny fragment of Poutini, for he could not bear to be parted altogether from his prized possession.

"What have you seen in the far-off land?" he was asked when he returned. He smiled and told them wonderful stories of birds called moas which were the size of many men, and of greenstone buried in a cold mountain stream, and of fantails and kererus, of fabulous white herons, and of trees which blazed with scarlet blooms like fire. He took the fragment of Poutini from its hiding place and fashioned axes and pendants and told them that in the southern island there was more hard greenstone to gladden their hearts.

It was stories such as these, spreading from village to village, which finally brought the Maoris to Aotearoa.

Te Wahi Pounamu

The South Island of New Zealand was assuredly Te Wahi Pounamu – The Place of Greenstone. But who can say, without shadow of doubt, how the pounamu came to this land of the south? Did Ngahue bring it with him and hide it in the river, or as some say, did Hine-tu-a-hoanga send the green fish Poutini to pursue him until he took refuge in the river? They say that he travelled up the river in darkness which was lit only by the glowing summit of Tara-o-Tama with Poutini close behind him. The fish struggled up a cascade but failed to reach the top. The water turned it over and it fell on the rocks below, slipping into a deep pool. There, injured by the fall and exhausted by the long pursuit, it died and its body turned into a mass of greenstone which gave its name to the west coast, and indeed to the whole of the South Island.* A bad-tempered fish was Poutini, too. Boys who give way to temper are rebuked by the saying, "Ha! a descendant of Poutini!"

---

* Ngahue did well to flee from Hine's green fish. Fifty years ago it was estimated that greenstone deposit at Tara-o-Tama alone amounted to more than a million tons.

Tama paddled through the
towering walls of the sounds.

Tangiwai is the loveliest kind of greenstone, clear and shining, with tear drops embedded in the stone. It is a water of weeping, and perhaps the stories of Ngahue and Poutini are but fables of the misty time before time, for there is another tale which must be told. It is the story of Tangiwai and Tama-ki-te-rangi.*

It was in later years, after the Maoris had begun to make their home in Aotearoa, that Tama was deserted by his three wives, Hine-kawakawa, Hine-kahurangi, and Hine-pounamu. No one knew where they had gone. Tama ranged vainly round the southern coasts. He called at Kaikoura where his crew found an abundance of succulent crayfish, naming the place Kai-koura-a-Tama-ki-te-rangi after the meal which Tama ate there.

Leaving Kaikoura he travelled round Murihiku, the end of the land, and sailed past the southern fiords. At Piopiotahi (Milford Sound) he heard a suspicious noise and paddled through the towering walls of the sound. There he found one of his wives turned into translucent greenstone. He bent over the cold body. The tears ran down his face and on to the hard stone, penetrating it until the tangiwai was flecked with tears.

Sorrow is for those who have departed, but life is for those who remain. Somewhere two other wives were waiting for their husband. Tama searched through every sound. His travelling cloak was torn to ribbons in the dense forest through which he passed, and the flax and kiekie and tangled shrubs of Fiordland have all sprung from the shreds of his tattered pokeka cloak.

Then he sailed northwards until, at the mouth of the Arahura River, he heard voices. They called him on, and the canoe followed the retreating song until it came to a waterfall and could go no further. The song was loud in his ears but he could find no signs of his wives. Little did he know that the boulders on which his hand had rested and the ledge beneath the water were the bodies of his wives and of their canoe, which had overturned in the singing river.

Tama abandoned his canoe and went sorrowfully on foot with his slave Tumu-aki until they came to the Kaniere Mountains. There they stopped and cooked birds for their evening meal, but Tumu-aki burnt his fingers and sucked them. In this way he

---

* The story is also related of Tamatea-pokai-whenua the great traveller.

destroyed his tapu, and for punishment he was turned into the mountain that bears his name; while tutaekoka, a variety of greenstone, was named to remind them of the birds they cooked.

Tangiwai, Kahurangi, Kawakawa, Tutaekoka, these are the names of different kinds of greenstone which were lost to Tama-ki-te-rangi when he searched for his runaway wives and failed to find them.

Kahurangi

It was the beautiful name borne by Tama's wife – Kahurangi. It means Mantle of the Skies. The name was also that of a renowned ancestress of a tribe that lived on the shore of the Hauraki Gulf. Her descendants became powerful and prosperous. They gloried in the strength of the hapu and believed that their success was due to their own prowess. They neglected the honour of the gods and forgot to perform the sacred rites.

The spirit of Kahurangi was sorrowful when she saw how proud her people had become. She came down from her home in the sky and entered one of the kaingas as a stranger. A tohunga and a faithful handful of people still observed some of the ancient ceremonies. They went to a stream, accompanied by Kahurangi, and chanted karakias. The ceremony concluded with the tohunga striking the surface of the water with a paddle. As he did so a bright light blossomed like fire round them and a rock appeared from the bed of the stream. When the light faded Kahurangi had disappeared, but the rock remained, dividing the stream.

For a time no one dared go near the mysterious rock which seemed to shine with an inner light. But one day an old woman, who was reputed to have unearthly powers, ventured to go close to it. She put out her hand and touched it. Immediately the sky darkened, thunder pealed overhead, forked lightning shot from the clouds and struck the rock, and it vanished. The clouds rolled away and the sun came out, shining on the waters that ran as they had done for so long before the coming of the rock. Everything was peaceful by the stream, but the old woman suffered unbearable pain in her arm. She stumbled through the bushes to a muddy lagoon and plunged into the water, throwing it over her head and body and praying to the gods. As suddenly as it had come the pain left her and she was filled with mana, with the life-giving power which came from Kahurangi. She ran back to the kainga and told the people. They laughed at her at first but when she showed them how she could run up trees faster than a boy, they realised that some mysterious power had come to her.

Even stranger things followed. Disease began to take some of the leading chiefs of the tribe, the crops suffered from drought and blight, and their enemies made sudden raids on them. Evil days had fallen upon the powerful Hauraki people.

The ariki and the rangatiras of the largest hapu went to a famous tohunga and begged him to ask the gods for help. All that night the tohunga prayed and called to the gods, using the words of the ancient karakias he had learnt in his young manhood. His voice rose and fell in an unearthly cadence, and the people trembled as they lay in their whares.

In the morning the tohunga called them to the marae.

"The gods have spoken," he said solemnly. "Tomorrow visitors will come to us. They are our own people. Amongst them is an old woman named Toke-whakatete who has passed under the shadow of the rock of Kahurangi. It is Toke who has caused your troubles. The gods have told me that our ancestress Kahurangi came back to us because of the love she bore us, and because she wanted to cure us of our boasting and evil ways. She took the shape of a rock, but this woman robbed it of its power, and now Kahurangi has departed. Some of her mana rests on Toke, but she is an evil woman.

"When the visitors arrive, keep a careful watch over her. The mana of Kahurangi rests in her arm. When night falls Toke will go to the stream to bathe the mana, and after that she will sit on a sandhill and make a ring of berries round her on the ground. As soon as she has finished you must seize her, gather up the berries, and take her to a whare where a fire is burning. Ask her to tell you her secret. If she refuses, drop the berries in the fire and hold up her arm. By the light of the flames as they burn the last berry you will see the mana of Kahurangi. Take a piece of bark from a rata tree and hold it to her arm, and in this way the mana will be captured. My children, if you do these things and treasure that mana-impregnated bark, you will eventually prosper in all you do."

The tohunga raised his hands in blessing on his people and fell to the ground. When they went to him they found that the gods had taken his wairua to themselves.

His words were remembered, and when the relatives came the next day, Toke-whakatete was followed. At dusk, as the last of the berries flared up in the fire, the mana of Kahurangi was transferred to the rata bark, and was buried in sacred ground.

The same night the ariki held counsel with the elders of the tribe. "I have had a dream," he told them. "There is a chief among the visitors, and he must wed my daughter and take her away. It is necessary for the prosperity of our tribe. Through the child that will be born to them the mana of Kahurangi will return to us and we will be strong again."

The next morning the ariki died, and the marriage ceremony was held over his body. At night the bride was restless and depressed, and the young husband asked what was troubling her.

"I have had a dream," she said. "The spirit of my father appeared to me and told me to dig up the rata bark."

When the sun rose again the two of them went with some of their friends to gather shellfish and fern-root as offerings to the gods. The young woman's hair was cut off with a flake of obsidian and the thick locks laid on the ground. The bark was uncovered, lifted out, and placed on the bride's head. She screamed with pain, and when the bark was removed it was found that the rest of her hair had been burnt, leaving her scalp smooth and white.

"It is a sign that the spirit still lives in the bark," they whispered to each other, and placed it in an elaborately carved waka.

"Take this with you as you journey," they said. "It will preserve you from harm and guide you on your way."

They returned to the pa and the chief and his wife began their wanderings. They climbed mountains and crossed wide plains, waiting for the gods to guide them. Long months of cold and heat went by. The woman became weary and ill, but when her husband went to get her a drink, he could find no water. The night was dark, and he could not see an arm's length in front of him. Sitting down beside his wife, he felt stones under his hand and began to throw them idly about him. They made a dull thud on the ground or crashed through leaves and twigs; but one stone made a gurgling sound as it fell.

"Water!" he cried. As he lifted his wife in his arms the moon came from behind the shoulder of the mountain and revealed a tiny lake hidden among the trees. The chief laid his wife down on the grassy edge and bathed her head. She revived and felt strong and well again. They threw a cluster of titoki leaves into the water as an offering to the spirit of the lake. A shaft of light suddenly shone on their faces from a crevice in the rocks. They tried to lift the casket which contained the bark, but it had become so heavy that it could not be moved. The light went out, the moon was hidden by clouds, and in the darkness they heard the crying of a baby. The woman clasped her husband's hand tightly and whispered, "Pray to the gods for me."

She waded through the water and stood under the rock where the light had appeared. As she gazed upwards she saw the face of the old tohunga. Tears ran down the tattooed furrows of his cheeks.

"My child, your courage has been rewarded. This is the birth-place of Kahurangi, and it is her voice you have heard. Her life-force lives in you now. Sorrow will come, and great joy, and through them our people will be restored."

There had been no feasting or games in the pa. Anxiously the guardians of the watch-tower searched each day for the returning of the young chief and his wife. There was rejoicing when they appeared, but little was said, for the shadow of evil still lay over the tribe.

A few days later, in a violent storm, a daughter was born to the daughter of the ariki. For six days she lived, a tiny mite whose cries were drowned by the never-ending storm. On the sixth day the lightning blazed incessantly and the child seemed bathed in liquid fire; and on the seventh day her spirit slipped from her body and was taken to the home of the gods.

There was no sign of the baby. In its place there lay a piece of greenstone, clear as the sacred lake, and shaped like a tear.

"It is the spirit of our baby and the mana of our ancestry," the young woman said through her tears. "It is Kahurangi herself, our baby, and the peace and prosperity of our tribe!"

While Kahurangi is treasured, the pride and mana of that tribe of Hauraki will never grow dim, for it came through weeping and sorrow and shame, and was restored by love.

28

Stories of Fish

The Shellfish which carried a Love Token
A tiny shellfish once bore a message of love from the East Coast to the Bay of Plenty. On a visit to relatives who lived at the Bay of Plenty a young man had seen a dark-skinned, brown-eyed, black-haired girl who lived at Opape, and had fallen in love with her. Not having the swift decision of Tutanekai or of Ponga, he returned to his home near Gisborne with his love undeclared, not even knowing whether the girl had noticed him among the other visitors.

At night, as he tossed on his sleeping mat, and by day in the forest snaring birds, and in canoes on fishing expeditions, his thoughts turned towards her. The long, winding Waioeka Gorge was the only highroad through the mountains, and there a lonely traveller might fall prey to his enemies. The route round the coast was long and hazardous, and he had no canoe of his own. His yearning spirit at length devised a way by which a message of love could be carried to her.

He chose a shellfish from the beach and, whispering to it in the quiet hours of the night, he threw it into the sea with a prayer that it might reach the loved one and pass on his message.

The little shellfish was tossed to and fro by the waves. It sank and rose again. A current from the south bore it on its way, past East Cape, and into the warmer waters of the Bay of Plenty. By swimming and crawling along the rocks it eventually reached Opape, and lay on the sand.

That day, or the next, the young woman went down to the beach to gather pipis and mussels for food. She picked up the little shellfish and then threw it away because it was so small. Somehow it managed to get near her again as she moved along the beach. Several times it was picked up and discarded, not only on that day, but the next and the next.

The young woman hung
the shellfish round her neck.

Presently she came to recognise it by some special markings on the shell. Wherever she turned it seemed to be under her hand, and no matter how often she threw it away, it returned. She realised that there was something peculiar about a shellfish which came back every time it was thrown away and to humour it, or to put an end to its persistence, she threaded it with a wisp of flax and hung it around her neck.

There was no one to tell her how dangerous the shellfish was to her maidenhood. The shellfish sang a song without words, without tune, that entered her breast and filled her heart with longing and love. She remembered the young man of Titirangi hill who had danced in the house of amusement some months before. She was in love with him, she longed for him, she could not live without him.

"You must go to him now, now, now," whispered the little shellfish.

We do not know how she went – whether the young man came part of the way to meet her, whether she persuaded her father to take her by canoe, or whether she toiled over the ranges, alone or in company. What is far more important, she reached her goal and was united to her lover because the little shellfish had carried out its task so well.

How Eels came down to Earth

In the beginning of time when the heaven and earth were first created, many different kinds of eels and fish lived in the cool waters of the second overworld, in the spring Puna-kau-ariki. Tane fashioned the sun as an ornament for Rangi; the years went by and Maui harnessed the sun to the sky and made him travel slowly across the arch of the heavens.

More years passed and the waters of Rangi-tamaku, the second heaven, were heated by the sun and evaporated, so that the overworld was full of vapour, and the springs dried up. Water-plants grew and covered the steaming surface waters, and there was no place where eels could live in comfort.

They decided to go down to earth. There were Para the barracouta, Tuere the blind eel, Mango the shark, Inanga the whitebait, Piharau the lamprey, Tuna the eel, and Ngoiro the conger eel. Their descent was hurried by Matuku the bittern, who could see them clearly in the shallow water, and gave them no rest as he hunted them through the water-weeds.

On their way down through the heaven above the heaven they met Tawhaki, who was climbing up in search of his wife.

"Why are you leaving your home?" he asked, and they told him that their world had become parched, and they feared the sharp beak of Matuku.

"Is Papa, the earth you have left, a fitting place for us?"

"All is well," Tawhaki replied. "There are streams and lakes, swamps and seas of cool water, and room for you all."

At first they took refuge in the streams, but Para became vicious and attacked Tuna, who fled to the swamps and deep water holes. Then Para took Ngoiro and Tuere with him and swam out to sea, where he lives in the great ocean of Kiwa.

Tuere, the blind eel, who is also called the hagfish, and is loathsome and slimy, had a parting word for Tuna. "Stay in your repulsive swamps," he said. "There you will be caught by the children of Tu and cooked for food."

Tuna was angry. "Go to the sea if you want. I warn you that you will become food for Mango the shark" – and so it proved to be, for the shark is the only fish that will eat the blind eel.

Piharau the lamprey burrowed under the shingle banks, and Inanga the whitebait departed for the shallows to save himself from the hungry mouths of Para, Ngoiro, and Mango. Even Tuna was not safe, for Matuku the bittern followed him, and still preys on him in the endless swamps of Papa-tu-a-nuku.

Kuku and Pipi

Kuku the mussel and Pipi the cockle were at enmity, they and their families. They shared the beach at Onetahua, and it was there that the battled raged. The pipis dug themselves into the sand and held their pa against the attack of the kukus. The mussels advanced in ranks, thrusting at their foes with their tongues, but they became clogged with sand and had to retire to the rocks at the end of the beach. That is the reason why cockles burrow in the sand and mussels cling to the rocks.

Te Pu-whakahara and Taka-aho, who are the fathers of whales and sharks, heard about the quarrel, and were vastly amused at the antics of the little people. Te Pu-whakahara asked what they were fighting about.

"They are fighting for possession of the beach," Taka-aho said.

"We should give them something to fight about. Our children are hungry, and they would make a tasty meal for them. Let us attack them now."

"It would be of no use," Taka-aho replied. "They would retire behind their sand defences."

Te Pu still thought that a sudden attack would provide a meal for his children, and Taka-aho led his followers in a rush up the beach. The pipis flew from them as swiftly as birds and burrowed into the sand so quickly that they were lost to sight in a moment. The whales were stranded on the beach. Their gills filled with sand and they died. The story must be true. Have we not all seen or heard of stranded whales which have come ashore to continue the conflict, and have been left behind by the receding tide?

Tutara-kauika the Chief of Whales

Women and children, and even grown men, kept well away from the big rock called Toka-a-houmea because it was the tuahu, the altar and sacred place of the old tohunga Te Tahi-o-te-rangi. He was a man to be feared, a killer at a distance, practised in black magic, and a familiar of evil spirits.

For long they had wished that he would fall victim to the powers of darkness, but the aged tohunga flourished and overcame his enemies by the power of his mind and the influence of Whiro the evil one.

"We must kill him, but it will need cunning and careful planning," the rangatiras said. They sat long into the night, weaving a plot as skilfully and patiently as a woman at work on a taniko pattern.

When daylight came they prepared their canoes for a sea voyage, laying in stores of food and water. A messenger was sent to Te Tahi to tell him that the men of the tribe were going on a mutton-bird hunting expedition to Whakaari, or White Island, the volcanic island in the Bay of Plenty, and that they needed him as their tohunga to protect them on the voyage, and to perform the sacred rites before the hunt began. It was a long time since Te Tahi had been invited to share in communal activities, and he accepted the invitation.

He was placed in the seat of honour in the largest canoe, and the fleet went down the river and into the open sea. A light breeze filled the sails, and by late afternoon they beached on the steaming shores of Whakaari.

Some of the men were left behind to guard the canoes while the hunters went off to seek the titi. Te Tahi accompanied a group of leading chiefs, who scrambled along the edge of the pohutukawa-lined cliffs round to the north-east side of the island, where they found a cave in which to spend the night. As soon as it was dark torches were lit, and the men caught the mutton-birds as they sat in their shallow burrows and holes, dazzled by the light. It was a strange sight with the smoky, flaring torches lighting the steaming soil, and the birds sitting motionless with staring eyes, waiting to be caught by the hunters. Before long each man had obtained a good catch of birds, which were taken back to the cave. Because of his tapu, Te Tahi lay down well away from the others and, tired after his unusual exertion, went to sleep.

As the shadows of the cave were softened by the first light of dawn, Te Tahi awoke and listened for a while to the tumble of the waves on the rocks below. There was no other sound. A sardonic smile crossed his face. The hunters were evidently still exhausted. He turned over and raised himself on his elbow to look at them. Close at hand he saw his bundle of titi birds, but they were the only things in the cave. There were no other heaps of birds, and no other men.

He scrambled to his feet and ran outside. A horrible thought entered his head. He rushed along the cliffs, pulling himself past dangerous places, until he came in sight of the beach where they had landed the previous afternoon. There was no sign of men or canoes there. He raised his eyes and saw, at some distance, the canoes gliding across the still water and the spreading arrows of their wakes. Faintly there came to his ears the song that gave the time to the paddlers.

A gust of wind brought a sulphur-laden cloud of smoke across the shore, blocking out his view of the dwindling canoes, and making him cough violently. He could feel the ground trembling beneath his feet. There was no water anywhere on the island, the calabashes had been taken, and already he was thirsty. But Te Tahi was not without resources, even though he had been marooned on a volcanic island. Grimacing in the heat, he took three blades of flax from his girdle. They were a powerful aid in his magic arts, for he had plucked them from a sacred flax bush which grew near his home. He stood at the edge of the cliff, waving the leaves and chanting a very old and potent karakia. Tangaroa the sea god heard the prayer, and sent Tutara-kauika, the ariki and rangatira of whales, to his aid.

Te Tahi saw the huge black shape emerge from the sea where deep water lies close to the shore. He hurried down to the beach, wrapped the flax leaves in his girdle, and swam out to the whale. As he reached it the huge creature submerged, and when it rose gently from the water again, Te Tahi was safely ensconced in the hollow on its back. It turned and swam south to the mainland at the Whakatane harbour mouth, its slave whale following in its wake.

They made a detour and were not seen by the returning titi hunters in the canoes. The tohunga left the whales at the mouth of the estuary, swam up the river, and walked across to his home. He rested there for a while until he knew that the canoes would be returning. After they landed they would have to pass his sacred rock Toka-a-houmea. He sat down in front of it, holding the tapu flax leaves in his hands, and watched the rangatiras and commoners of the tribe filing past. They had seen him as they dragged the canoes ashore, but there was no escape.

They did not dare to look directly at the old tohunga, but walked past with heads averted, while Te Tahi looked at them with grim amusement. He did not trouble them long with his presence, but went to live at Matata. When he died he became a marakihau or god of the sea, and was doubtless able to thank Tutara-kauika in his own language for his rescue from the perils of the volcanic island.

Pelorus Jack

Even in the brief period of Pakeha history in New Zealand there have been a few events which have already begun to assume a legendary aura. A recent one is to be found in the antics of Opo, the tame dolphin of Opononi; another, even more famous, is that remarkable character Pelorus Jack, the dolphin* of Pelorus Sound. It is history and not legend that tells how Pelorus Jack met steamers and escorted them through Admiralty Bay as far as French Pass, and that a special act of Parliament was passed in order to protect him.

Legend can go further back in time and recount more wonderful deeds than any history. It is legend that tells us that two men loved one girl. She chose one of them for her husband and the rejected lover, Ruru, who was a powerful man, seized the girl and threw her over the edge of a cliff. Her husband had seen this dreadful deed, and he attacked Ruru, but was overpowered and in turn thrown on to the ugly rocks below, where his spirit joined that of his young wife and journeyed to the Reinga (the departing place of spirits).

Full of pride, Ruru climbed down to the beach to inspect the mangled bodies of the lovers. His attention was attracted by a grey body rising from the waves. He was startled for a moment, and then realised that it was a dolphin, and cursed it. The words he used were those of an ancient enchantment which he had once overheard, and were so powerful that the dolphin was killed, and its body floated ashore.

These events, unknown, to Ruru, had been watched by a tohunga, who came down to the beach and accused him of killing the young people, and of using an enchantment which was reserved for those who were students of the whare-wananga (the school of learning).

"You have desecrated the gods, and wantonly destroyed your fellow beings, their fairest creation," the tohunga told him. "You cannot escape punishment."

By this time Ruru's arrogance had vanished. He cringed before the tohunga's anger, but the priest was implacable.

"Here lies the dead body of this dolphin. I command your spirit to depart from you and to enter the fish. You must never leave this coast, but devote yourself to good deeds, and escort the canoes as

---

* Properly Risso's dolphin, the only one of its species to be seen in New Zealand waters.

The dolphin of Pelorus Sound.

they enter and leave the sound. Guide them and protect them until I release you."

Ruru's body fell to the ground, and at the same moment the dolphin stirred, contorted its body, and slithered back into the waves. Once every year, it is said, Ruru returned and begged the tohunga to release him from his long duty, but was bidden to go back and carry on his work. Eventually the tohunga grew old and died, and there was no one to take the curse from Ruru. Through the long years and the longer centuries the dolphin was the escort of the canoes of Pelorus Sound.

Then came the white man with his monstrous iron ships, and Ruru guided him through the waterways to French Pass as he had done to the canoes for so long.

Pelorus Jack has not been seen for many years. As the white man's mana grew stronger, the Maori gods grew weak. The curse may have worn thin and powerless with age, or it may have been dissipated by the white man's materialism. Who can tell? We can only hope that Ruru has expiated his crimes of long ago and found peace in the placid waters of the sound.

Bibliography

Maori Religion and Mythology; Elsdon Best.

Polynesian Mythology; Sir George Grey.

Legends of the Maori; James Cowan and Sir Maui Pomare.

Revenge; John White.

The Lore of the Whare-wananga; S. Percy Smith.

Old Tasman Bay; J. D. Peart.

Myths and Legends of Polynesia; Johannes C. Andersen.

Tuhoe; Elsdon Best.

Legends of the Maori; Colonel T. W. R. Porter.

Te Ika a Maui; Richard Taylor.

Te Whanganui; T. W. Downes.

Tikao Talks; Herries Beattie.

Maori Lore of Lake, Alp and Fiord; Herries Beattie.

Folk Tales of the Maori; A. A. Grace.

Maori Place Names; Johannes C. Andersen.

Te Tohunga; W. Dittmer.

Journal of the Polynesian Society.

Transactions of the New Zealand Institute.

The Ancient History of the Maori, Volumes 1 and 2; John White.

The Coming of the Maori; Sir Peter Buck.

Legends of Rotorua; A. W. Reed.

The Maori, Volume One; Elsdon Best.

Ponga and Puhihuia; H. J. Fletcher.

Fairy Folk Tales of the Maori; James Cowan.

Glossary

ariki: chief or leader.

atua: god.

haka: dance; frequently a war-dance.

hapu: sub-tribe.

kainga: unfortified village

kaka: bird – a kind of parrot.

karakia: spell of incantation.

kehua: ghost.

kiwi: bird – a wingless bird.

ko: a tool for digging.

korari: the flower stem of the flax. It is very light.

kumara: sweet potato.

kuri: dog.

makutu: magic.

mana: influence, power, authority or prestige.

manuka: shrub or tree, often called tea-tree.

marae: courtyard or open space in the village.

mere: a short, flat weapon made of greenstone.

moko: tattooing.

ngarara: monster reptile.

pa: fortified village.

pakeha: white man.

patu: weapon.

patupaiarehe: fairy.

patupatu: weapon.

poi: light ball attached to a string, and twirled rhythmically to the accompaniment of a song or dance.

ponaturi: sea fairies.

puhi: unmarried girl.

putara: a trumpet made of a shell with a wooden mouthpiece.

rakaunui: chief.

rangi: the sky or sky-father.

reinga: the spirit-land, or leaping place of spirits.

taiaha: weapon about five feet long, made of hard wood.

tane: man.

taniwha: monster.

tapu: sacred, forbidden.

taro: cultivated plant used for food.

taua: war party.

tekoteko: carved figure on the gable of a house.

tipua: goblin or demon.

titi: mutton-bird.

toa: warrior.

tohunga: priest.

toetoe: long-leaved plant with lofty plumes.

totara: forest tree.

tuahu: a sacred place in the village.

turehu: fair-skinned fairy people.

wahine: woman.

wairua: soul or spirit.

waka: canoe; carved trough or casket.

whare: house.

whata: food store.